Advance Praise for *Footsteps of Federer*

"*Footsteps of Federer* is a brilliant book, a creative idea, a travelogue, a why-tennis-matters manifesto, a thoughtful essay on Roger Federer, and a personal story of why things matter to us and what matters most. Stay for the goosebumps-inducing end."

—GREG BISHOP, *Sports Illustrated*

"Dave Seminara has deftly combined his love of travel with his love of tennis to tell us how one of the world's most beautiful countries produced one of the world's most popular athletes."

—THOMAS SWICK, author of *The Joys of Travel*

"You would think that everything has already been written about Roger Federer, the greatest tennis player of all time. But Seminara's redemptive travels around Switzerland introduce us to sights, courts, and characters that reveal new layers to the Federer story. His sense of humor, love of tennis, and willingness to ask anyone anything make Seminara's pilgrimage a fun ride you'll want to take."

—MEGAN FERNANDEZ, *Indianapolis Monthly*

"The crux of this story is one writer's devotion to the most beloved tennis athlete in history. To me it was also a beautiful trip down memory lane. I played in the German Bundesl͟i͟ ͟ ͟ ͟ ͟ ͟ ͟rs after

retiring from the tour and Dave's description of the little tennis clubs he visited on his journey captures the joy of post match dinners and draft beer that I remember so fondly."

—CLIFF DRYSDALE, Hall of Fame tennis player
and ESPN broadcaster

"A charming new book about all things Federer that concludes with a plot twist worthy of one of Hercule Poirot's drawing-room denouements."

—SIMON BRIGGS, *Daily Telegraph*

"In a creative and thoughtful way, Dave Seminara digs both wide and deep into tennis great Roger Federer's native Switzerland."

—JOEL DRUCKER, Tennis.com-Tennis Channel, author
of *Jimmy Connors Saved My Life*, and historian-at-large,
International Tennis Hall of Fame

Footsteps
of Federer

**A Fan's
Pilgrimage Across
7 Swiss Cantons in 10 Acts**

DAVE SEMINARA

Post Hill
PRESS

A POST HILL PRESS BOOK
ISBN: 978-1-64293-856-2
ISBN (eBook): 978-1-64293-857-9

Footsteps of Federer:
A Fan's Pilgrimage Across 7 Swiss Cantons in 10 Acts
© 2021 by Dave Seminara
All Rights Reserved

Cover art by Chad Lowe

This is a work of nonfiction. All people, locations, events, and situations are portrayed to the best of the author's memory.

Post Hill Press
New York • Nashville
posthillpress.com

Published in the United States of America
1 2 3 4 5 6 7 8 9 10

Contents

Preface 5

DAY ONE: Fay-day-rare Will Live Here? 9

DAY TWO: I Am Federer Too 15

DAY THREE: Father Federer and the Dark Forest 23

DAY FOUR: What Kind of Fool would Prevent Roger
Federer from Building a Tennis Court? 37

DAY FIVE: "You Will Shower in the Same Place
Roger Showered" 47

DAY SIX: "For Roger, We Would Wait All Night" 61

DAY SEVEN: "The Charmest, Most Sympathetic,
Most Interesting Sports Man in the World" 73

DAY EIGHT: If There's a $48 Cheeseburger on the Menu,
You Might Bump into Robert Federer and the Twins 89

DAY NINE: Bigger Than Erasmus 99

DAY TEN: Mirka Has Beautiful Teeth 107

EPILOGUE 125

Federer Family Milestones in Switzerland 129
Acknowledgments 137
About the Author 139

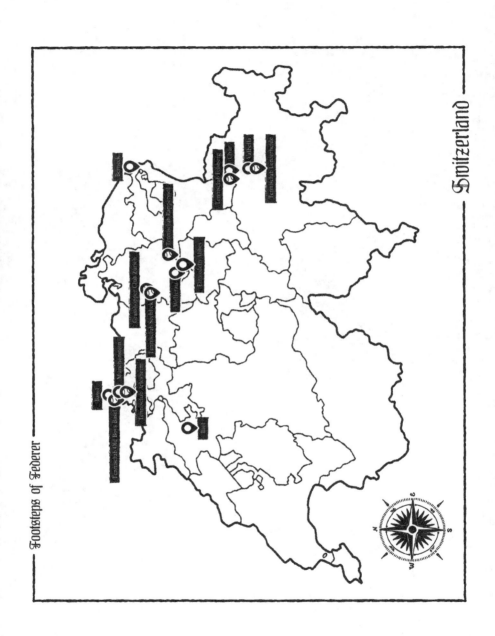

Footsteps of Federer

Switzerland

Preface

The Einsiedeln Abbey has been an important place of pilgrimage since shortly after St. Meinrad, the Martyr of Hospitality, retreated to the secluded "Dark Forest" in a valley between Lake Zürich and Lake Lucerne to establish a hermitage around 835. I visited in October 2019 as part of an unusual pilgrimage: I had come to Switzerland to walk, and hopefully play tennis, in the footsteps of Roger Federer, and I wanted to start my journey in an appropriately auspicious place.

But when I contacted the abbey to arrange my visit, the Benedictine monks had a surprise for me. "Did you know our abbot is also named Federer?" asked Marc Dosch, the abbey's lay representative. I had not. "Yes, and he baptized Roger's children." I resisted the urge to say, *well, I'll be damned,* and Dosch casually mentioned that Abbot Urban Federer would also be attending the final of the Swiss Indoors, the tennis tournament in Basel that I was building my Federer pilgrimage around. Destiny, indeed.

I've been a tennis player and obsessive fan since the late 1970s when I idolized Björn Borg, and later John McEnroe, Boris Becker and, most of all, Roger. Health problems forced me to give up playing tennis for long spells, first in late 2004 (multiple sclerosis attack) and again in 2015 (knee surgery). In January 2017, just as my knee was almost healed, I was diagnosed with morphea, a painful autoimmune skin disease that attacked my feet, legs, torso, and arms.

By the time I started to plan my Federer trip, I had progressed from the dark times, when my skin was so itchy and brittle that standing in place for more a couple minutes was excruciating, to a point where I was dreaming about playing tennis again. And not just on neighborhood courts, but somewhere special, somewhere Roger had played, as a little treat to myself for all the suffering I had endured over the last few years.

The travel editor of *The New York Times* commissioned me to write an (all too brief) story, which covered some of my expenses for a ten-day trip, and my credential application for the Swiss Indoors was approved, which meant that I'd hopefully have a chance to ask Roger questions in post-match press conferences. I have a couple of friends who are almost as obsessed with Roger as I am, but alas, neither were free, so I resolved to go alone.

Why should a happily married man of forty-seven years with two kids obsess over a Swiss tennis player? My Fed fetish began with simple appreciation for Roger's beautiful game: the graceful strokes, his balletic footwork, his bold net game, his mastery of every shot in the sport's canon. Over the years, though, his beautiful game became less important to me compared to what I've come to admire most about the Swiss legend—his sportsmanship, his sense of humor, and his willingness to show weakness and shed tears on the court. I like the man so much I tried to name my second-born child after him. (My wife vetoed that plan, and a few years later, Roger named one of his sons Leo, the name we picked for our firstborn.)

I've had opportunities to ask Roger questions in press conferences at tournaments I've covered, but I'd never properly met him until 2013. That year, I was covering Wimbledon for *The New York Times* during the first week of the tournament when Roger lost to Sergiy Stakhovsky, then ranked 116th, in the second round. On the first Monday morning of the fortnight, during the gloriously quiet hour or two before the grounds of the All England Club are open to the public, I was walking and talking with Nick Bollettieri when I saw Roger and Paul Annacone, his coach at the time, approaching us.

Roger made a beeline toward us and embraced Nick. For a moment, I stood there, assuming the three of them would have a chat while I stood there feeling like a discarded milk carton. But Roger came to the rescue, turning to me with a friendly greeting and a handshake. Our interaction lasted no more than a minute, but he was very nice, nothing extraordinary, but that was the beauty of it, he acted like a normal, genuine person, not at all like a celebrity. I'm not easily starstruck, but I returned to the media center feeling like I'd just received a blessing from the Pope.

My admiration for Mr. Roger (no middle name) Federer reached new levels in 2017 when he won two majors after nearly every tennis writer had already written his tennis obit. He could have quietly drifted off to the Alps to meditate in the lotus position while counting his Swiss francs, but instead, he rededicated himself to the sport and turned the tables on his younger rivals.

When Roger won the Australian Open in 2017—his first major in nearly five years—I had just started to experience out-of-control inflammation in my feet and legs. The condition was so painful and itchy that I couldn't sleep. Staying up all night watching Roger win Down Under brightened my mood and eased the pain.

2019 was a year of transition for me—and I've had several of these, having moved well over a dozen times across several countries and states since I graduated from college many years ago. At the time I was planning my Federer trip, we had just moved from Oregon to Florida, where I hoped that the warm and humid climate would help my brittle skin. With the decade winding down, I was also frustrated with my writing career and was thinking about a change.

Big life decisions are always a perfect excuse for a trip, and I reckoned that traveling across seven cantons to the neighborhoods where Roger has lived and the tennis clubs where he's honed his game before watching him play at his hometown tennis tournament would help me better understand not just Roger but also Switzerland, that prosperous, heartbreakingly beautiful but enigmatic four-language outlier in the heart of Europe. With any luck, I could also make my tennis comeback on hallowed ground.

Day One

Fay-day-rare Will Live Here?

After an overnight transatlantic flight and a layover of a few hours in Frankfurt, I stepped off the plane in Zürich and into a long tunnel in the terminal bleary eyed, feeling a bit like a zombie caught between time zones working on zero hours' sleep. The first person I saw was Roger Federer, looking dapper in an expensive suit. He was on a monitor, walking across the screen in a loop. "Hello and welcome to Basel," he said with a smirk before pausing and, with that wonderful childlike grin he has, continuing, "Just kidding, of course this is Zürich, enjoy your stay." It was an ad for Credit Suisse, which is probably a lot better at banking than it is at humor.

It would have been better if Roger had turned up at the airport to greet me, but this was the next best thing.

I chose Rapperswil, a charming small town of about seven thousand moneyed and well-coiffed residents on the western shore of Lake Zürich, as my first Swiss base because Federer had recently purchased an eighteen-thousand-square-meter plot of land to build (yet another) dream home on Lake Zürich, just outside Rapperswil town limits, for a reported $40–$50 million. I resisted the urge to sleep and spent a couple of hours exploring the town on foot before setting off to look at Roger's land.

It was easy to see why Roger and his family would want to live in Rapperswil. It's a quiet, idyllic little place, with a medieval castle, a fine harbor with expensive-looking boats, a venerable monastery, and meandering, cobblestone streets with attractive shops and overpriced restaurants that are perfectly fine if you're Roger Federer but not so appealing for the budget traveler.

Outside Rapperswil's monastery, which dates to 1606, I heard a chorus of angelic voices and snuck in to observe some locals engaging in a sung mass in German.

Rapperswil ©Dave Seminara

I said a short prayer, asking for good health, and took off by bike along a surprisingly busy road that curls north and west of town, hugging the lake as it passes through Kempraten, a village that's only a kilometer or so outside Rapperswil.

The homes along the lake side of the road I pedaled along are a mix of massive, garish modern homes and classier century-old affairs. It's a prosperous area, perfect for a bank manager who commutes to Zürich or a twenty-time major tennis champion, but one could easily drive by Roger's property without giving it a second look. I expected it to be more secluded, tucked away somewhere with armed guards or a high wall.

But it was easy to find—I saw a large vacant piece of land, along with bulldozers, piles of rubble and construction equipment and suspected I was in the right place. Roger's next-door neighbor-to-be was cutting his lawn on a riding mower. I flagged the man down and introduced myself.

He shook my hand and said his name was Louis. He had the rugged hands of someone who made his living with his hands, and his home was lovely but looked old and perhaps in need of a fresh coat of paint and the odd repair. I wondered if perhaps his family had lived here for generations, but Louis spoke no English so there was no way for me to find out. "Is Roger Federer moving in next door to you?" I asked, feeling a bit foolish as he remained seated on his riding mower.

He didn't understand me, so I played charades, whacking an imaginary Federer forehand in the air with my hand, and repeated, "Roger Federer will live here?" a bit louder, as though that might increase his English comprehension. (Americans have an unfortunate habit of speaking louder rather than simply learning other useful languages.) The man still looked confused so I showed him a backhand and repeated the name Federer, wondering if I'd have

to run through the canon of shots—overhead, serve, drop shot, or even a tweener—before he'd understand me.

I had come to Switzerland hoping to play some tennis on a real court, not tennis charades on the street. "Oh, Fay-day-rare," he said very slowly as though he was talking to, well, what's the correct terminology these days for someone who used to be called mentally retarded? He made quite a floor show of correcting my pronunciation.

I nodded apologetically and said, "Yes, yes." The American pronunciation of Federer must sound so peculiar to Swiss ears that it's barely recognizable.

The Swiss press had been reporting on a local pseudo controversy involving Switzerland's spatial planning laws, which designate all of the country's lakes and rivers public. It's a matter of dispute whether the law includes riverbanks and lakeshores, but it's generally understood that landowners aren't supposed to block access to rivers and lakes. Swiss media outlets reported that Roger was planning to build a tennis court on his property but no footpath, and some were insisting that Roger should provide access to the lake just like anyone else.

The idea that Roger should have to allow people to traipse across his property seems ridiculous to me, but it's an interesting issue because it cuts across three important pillars of Swiss culture: privacy, access to public lands, and the notion that the rights of one person, even a famous one, can't supersede anyone else's. I wanted to ask Louis how he felt about this, but we were reduced to playing charades, grinning at each other and making gestures like idiots.

I didn't trespass onto Roger's property, obviously, but I could see that he's going to have an epic view. The property is around the bend from Rapperswil, so from his lawn, and presumably his tennis court, he'll have a panoramic view across the lake at Rapperswil's castle and old town with towering snow-capped mountains looming to the south.

I spent an hour and a half tromping around Rapperswil's atmospheric streets looking for a reasonable place to eat dinner, but I discovered that it's easier to find Roger Federer's new home than a cheap meal in Rapperswil. A young woman with a nose ring at my hotel suggested I check out the Restaurant Quellenhof, but I discovered that their cheapest entrée was calf liver, which I wouldn't eat for free, let alone for $43.

I almost ate at a Thai restaurant, but the prospect of paying $35 for pad Thai felt about as appetizing as cleaning a baboon cage, so I ventured out of Rapperswil's center, across the railroad tracks in search of Tennisclub Rapperswil. I was hoping to find someone to talk tennis with, but it was a cool, damp evening near the end of the outdoor tennis season, and there were no players about.

A trio of Sicilians, who spoke just a bit of English, were there running a little club café/restaurant, but there were no customers. I got a heaping portion of tasty penne Bolognese for $15, a pretty sweet deal by Swiss standards. It was the first of several meals I was to enjoy at tennis clubs in Switzerland. As it turns out, tennis clubs are often the best place in town to find an affordable meal in this nation of handsomely compensated professionals.

Two of the Sicilians were quite friendly even though we shared no common language, save my kindergarten-level Italian. The woman, who was bundled up as though she was prepared to trek in the Himalayas, said she hoped that Roger would come play at the club, but she hadn't seen him yet. The cook, on the other hand, seemed like he was pissed off at the world; he eyed me warily as he prepared my pasta, and I wondered what the hell his problem was. I would later learn from a Swiss broadcaster who plays tennis at the club that the man's son had just killed his wife and himself only weeks before.

I Am Federer Too

aves of dense, smoke-colored clouds bobbed over sloping mountaintops as my train skated east past villages punctuated with onion-domed churches and tidy A-frame homes with decorative shutters. It was early on a Saturday morning and I was heading to Berneck, a country village of about four thousand people that hugs the Austrian border in St. Gallen canton, where the Federer clan originates from. I still felt like my body clock was somewhere near the Azores, but my spirit was feather-light. Travel has always been a life-affirming tonic for me. In my world, travel is freedom personified, and if you put me on a nice train or a ship headed *anywhere* life is just grand.

My trip to Berneck included two trains and a bus, but it began with the online Swiss phone directory before I left home. Federer is not a common name in Switzerland, but there are at least a few dozen Federers listed countrywide. Roger isn't in there, but his dad, Robert, is, and with a listed number no less. I wanted to verify that there were still Federers in Berneck, and, sure enough, there are lots of them. I noticed that one listing, for a Jakob Federer, also listed a @federer.org email domain.

I googled the name, wondering if perhaps he worked for Roger's foundation, but I discovered that Jakob Federer is a vintner and a consultant. I emailed him and he didn't respond. Then I sent him a message on LinkedIn, and sure enough, he got back to me and invited me to have lunch in his home.

If you had to take two trains and a bus anywhere in the United States, you'd be hard pressed to accurately predict your arrival time beyond perhaps letting loved ones know that you'd arrive sometime before Halley's Comet stops by our planet again. But I stepped off the bus across from Berneck's *Rathaus*, in the center of the village, at 9:43 a.m., the precise time the Swiss rail app predicted I would arrive. No one's going to mistake Switzerland for Suriname or Senegal anytime soon.

I had a few minutes to kill before my meeting with Jakob, so I poked around the center of this sleepy alpine village, which has one main drag with a few shops, clusters of brightly painted, old A-frame homes, and two churches, one Catholic and one Protestant. The place seemed deserted, but the church bells gonged ferociously, loud enough to be heard on the tops of the sloping green hills that stretch a bit higher than your average topspin lob above the town.

Jakob pulled up, right on time in a snazzy Volvo, and greeted me like a friend next to the Rathaus (town hall), which features a bust of the Swiss poet Heinrich Federer (1866–1928). Jakob appeared to be in his fifties; he had intelligent blue eyes, a salt-and-pepper beard and a small gold earring in his left ear. He had on a kind of Swiss variation on the Yorkshire flat cap and was dressed in a scarf for the morning's damp chill.

Jakob Federer in Berneck ©Dave Seminara

"So is Heinrich Federer one of Roger's ancestors?" I asked, as we walked up the steps toward the bust.

"I don't think so," he said. "Actually, he never lived here."

"So why is there a bust of him here?" I asked.

"You see, we are so close to the Austrian border here that during the war, the town felt that we should express strongly that we are Swiss, not Austrians, and he was like a symbol of being Swiss. It's like a marker for the place."

We explored the old Catholic church; Jakob told me that my ears hadn't deceived me, it had the third largest church bell in Switzerland. "They built this in the 1930s after the Protestant church got a loud bell, so the Catholics decided they needed to have an even louder bell to drown out the Protestants." Behind the Catholic Church, there's a small cemetery with quite a few Federer tombstones. Jakob said that there are about a hundred Federers in the village. Robert's grandmother, Käthi, is buried in the cemetery, but

Berneck ©Dave Seminara

they only keep the headstones displayed for a few years, so it's no longer visible.

Jakob told me that he was a seminarian years ago but decided not to become a priest. I wasn't surprised—he seemed like the kind of sympathetic and kind person who might be the priest everyone in the parish adores.

Jakob Federer grew up in Berneck, left for quite a few years, and decided to come back and raise his (now-grown) children in Berneck, together with his wife, Antonia. "It's very quiet, a beautiful place," he said, as we ducked out of a light rain into his Volvo for a trip up into the hills above town to see his vineyard.

As we climbed up a snaking road above the town, Jakob confessed that he had no interest in Roger—or any sports, for that matter, besides cycling. He said that he didn't think he and Roger were relatives, at least not close ones.

"Has Roger been to Berneck?" I asked.

"He has," he said. "I don't know how long ago, though. He used to come here as a boy to visit his grandmother, I know that. And his father still comes to visit his friends from his school times."

The German word *feder*, Jakob explained, means feather or quill, and in the Middle Ages, Federers were scribes. Jakob is something of a Renaissance man in Berneck, he has a winery called Stegeler (Stairs), a consulting business, and he's the vice president of the village.

"So you're like the Mike Pence of Berneck?" I asked, smiling.

"You could say that," he said.

We stepped out of the car on a hill overlooking Berneck, which dates to 892, next to a barn.

"We picked our merlot grapes yesterday since you were coming today, so we need to check on them to see how they're drying," Jakob explained before we ate some of his delicious, crunchy seeded grapes that were drying in high-tech compartments inside the shed.

Jakob explained that there was a schism in the Federer clan after a great fire ravaged Berneck in 1848. One branch of the family was blamed and were expelled from the village. I told Jakob that I was meeting Abbot Federer the next day at Einsiedeln and he said, "Oh, he's from the Federer clan who were expelled from the village. My wife is related to him; tell him we said hi."

At the village wine cellar, Jakob Schmid Kaspar Wetli, our next stop, Jakob and a number of other local producers age their wines in giant oak barrels. The smell of the oak was literally intoxicating. If Jakob would've allowed me to pitch a tent in the cellar, I would have. We tasted a number of his wines and each one was better than the next, but there was something that didn't add up for me.

"Why name your winery Stegeler?" I asked. "Why not Federer?"

Jakob's grapes ©Jakob Federer

"No, no, I won't do this," he insisted.

"Is that because you can't use the Federer name as a product legally?" I asked.

"No, no, I could do it," he said. "After all, I am Federer too, so why not?"

"But wouldn't you sell a lot more wine if people recognized the Federer name?"

"I'm not trying to sell the most wine," he said, shrugging his shoulders as if to indicate that we were on different wavelengths. "I can only produce ten thousand bottles per year, and the focus is on quality."

On the way back to his home, an attached townhouse very close to the center of the village, we passed by a cavernous, hand-some Alpine-style home with brightly painted gray and black detail and the number 1586, indicating the year of construction,

Robert Federer's childhood home ©Dave Seminara

emblazoned in black paint. "That's the house Robert Federer grew up in," he said. It was a huge house, so I was curious if Robert had grown up with money. "No, no, it's not a house for one family, two or three families live there."

After we enjoyed a nice vegetarian lunch together with his wife, Antonia, in their home, Bruno Seelos, the village president, stopped by for a chat. As we munched on some of the best grapes I've ever eaten in my life, Bruno explained that the village planned to name something after Roger, but they were waiting until after he retired. The village has a bust of the Swiss poet Heinrich Federer in the town center, even though he never lived in the town, I pointed out. And so why not another one, I asked, or perhaps a statue? Jakob and Antonia weren't convinced this was necessary. "It's like a cult of personality," she said, dismissing the idea out of hand.

Bruno drove me to the train station and on the way told me that Jakob and Antonia are perhaps the only people in the village who see no reason to honor Roger. "He doesn't need an honor from Berneck," he said, as we drove the village's quiet main drag. "But it's also an honor for *us*, something for us to be proud of that he has a family connection to this little place."

Father Federer and
the Dark Forest

Ürich is a melancholy and lonely place on a cold autumn
Sunday morning. I took a train and two trams from
Rapperswil to a leafy suburb south of Zürich through
largely empty streets, where the only sounds were church bells,
chirping birds, and the rattling of trams on their tracks, to see the
Grasshopper tennis club, a venerable establishment where Roger
often trains.

I had to hike up a series of steep streets from the tram stop and
my Achilles screamed at me along the way. Using tidbits I picked
up from Rene Stauffer's Federer biography, *Quest for Perfection*,
tips from interviews, and other research, I identified a dozen or so
clubs around the country that I wanted to check out. At Grasshopper, I was scheduled to meet Marko Budic, a former professional
player who is a board member at the club. I had brought my tennis

gear in the hopes that we could hit some balls, but I wondered if my aching feet and legs were up to the task.

I arrived twenty minutes early for the meeting, and the club, situated next to a botanical garden in a neighborhood of million-franc mansions, was empty. There were five red clay courts and one hard court, and the club's logo—a small *Z* inside a larger *C* and an even bigger *G*—was meticulously sculpted into a grassy hill next to the courts. The front door to the club was open, and a collection of racquets—most with broken strings—were hung on a wall near the entrance. A plaque commemorating the upcoming (2023) one-hundred-year anniversary of the club adorned a wall near the door. There were hoppers full of balls and a neat stack of towels with the club logo in the unlocked vestibule. Apparently no one at the club was worried about theft or vandalism.

An old man with a dog stopped by and asked me a question I didn't understand in German. He repeated the question, as if I

Grasshopper Club ©Dave Seminara

might better understand his German on the second time around, to no avail. Growing frustrated, he walked into the vestibule of the club, reached into one of the hoppers and grabbed a tennis ball, which he then tossed for his dog. Apparently he wanted my permission to take a ball and then decided that he didn't need it.

Marko pulled up right on time in a dark, late-model BMW. We had to sit at a table outside in the fifty-degree chill to eat the pastries I brought because he didn't have the key to the club's café, which was closed for the season. A fit, tall man with short-cropped hair who looked fit enough to still be on the pro tour, Marko told me that he played on the ATP futures circuit in the nineties for three years. Now forty-three and working for Credit Suisse, he still plays tournaments.

"I'm ranked one-fifty in the country and number two for those above thirty-five," he said.

"Wait, you're number two for over-thirty-fives and Roger is number one?" I asked.

"No, no, Roger is not included in those rankings," he said. "But I did play him once, in doubles. It was in a challenger tournament back in 1997. He was playing with Yves Allegro at the time."

"Did you win?"

"No, no," he said laughing. "We lost."

"Too bad," I said. "It would be awesome to be undefeated against Roger."

"I know. Rog doesn't remember the match, but I do."

Budic said that when Roger wants to train on one of their clay courts, they usually put him on court 3, because it's the only court that stands alone.

"But it's funny, when he plays on the other courts, which have courts next to them, people don't use those courts," he said. "We

Grasshopper courts ©Dave Seminara

don't tell them they can't. They just don't. It's like they don't want their balls going on his court."

"It would be a little awkward to have to say, 'Hey, Roger, little help,' wouldn't it?"

"Absolutely," Budic said.

"Does he have someone schedule his court?" I asked.

"No, no, he calls direct for himself. He never asks for any special treatment either."

Budic explained that Grasshopper and many of the other top tennis clubs, including Old Boys in Basel, where Roger trained as a kid, play in a highly competitive tennis league called the Interleague. "Roger played in this league as a kid until he was too good for it," he said. Grasshopper and some of the other top teams, including Seeblick, which had won the tournament two of the last three years and was next on my club hit list, paid top players to compete in what amounts to Switzerland's tennis equivalent of the Premier League.

I asked Budic what it was like when Roger practiced at the club and he said that "Rog," as he called him, tends to come at off hours on weekdays, when few people are around. "People are always asking me when will Roger be here, but we never tell them," he said. Budic said that kids ask him for autographs but they're respectful, they don't approach him until after he's done with his practice.

"This is why Roger likes to live in Switzerland," he said. "People give him space here."

"What does he do after practice, does he leave right away?" I asked.

"Not usually, no. He's very relaxed, many times he'll eat in our restaurant, have a coffee, talk to people. He drives himself too; he acts just like anyone else who plays tennis."

All the tennis talk had me primed to try to test my feet and legs on the court, but alas Budic hadn't brought his gear, so I would have to wait.

"How much does it cost to join this club, anyway?" I asked as we stood up to leave.

"It's very expensive," he said.

"How expensive?" I asked.

"It's a secret, actually I cannot say."

After he left, I grabbed one of the club towels with the fancy logo on it and stuffed it in my backpack, figuring it would be a nice souvenir for my sons. Then I immediately regretted it and thought about putting it back before realizing that they had a video camera in the place recording the scene. For a moment, I panicked, wondering what to do. Then I reconsidered, reckoning that a club that was so expensive that its membership fees were secret could probably afford to lose a towel.

Tennisclub Seeblick (Lake View in English) is a posh, idyllic little club of well-groomed red clay courts that's almost directly across Lake Zürich from the rival Grasshopper club. By the time I arrived, the sun had come out and there were a host of people playing tennis, including a pair of precocious teens, some middle-aged men playing doubles, and a foursome of beautifully dressed women who wouldn't have looked out of place on the cover of an upscale active living lifestyle magazine for seniors.

The views over the lake from the club café and from several of the courts justify paying $5 for an espresso, so I ordered one and sat outside watching the tennis as well as clusters of joggers parading back and forth on a lakeview path that fronted rows of mansions. The setting was dreamlike; I was surrounded by privileged people who, if reincarnation is real, were obviously Mother Teresa types in past lives to have earned this kind of lifestyle. I knew I didn't belong here, but I also felt like there was no better time than the present to start my tennis comeback.

I buttonholed a club member named Alan who was enjoying a post-match coffee at a high-top table next to mine. I explained my situation, showing him my swollen feet, which have roughly half the range of motion they should have and look perennially sunburned.

"You're going to play now in this condition?" he asked.

I nodded.

"You know, I couldn't play tennis for eighteen years because of my back, so I can relate to this problem," he said. "I have fifteen minutes if you want to try it."

I dashed down into the men's locker room, tearing off my clothes with all the excitement of a teenager about to lose his

TC Seeblick ©Dave Seminara

virginity. Alan sparred with me gently and although my timing was off, I felt a sense of exhilaration to be back on a tennis court, and not just any tennis court but an incredibly pretty tennis court at a club where Roger has trained.

I felt no pain during my fifteen minutes on the court because it was glorious to be hitting tennis balls again. It was mind over body, and I felt nothing but joy. But my feet were angry with me for the rest of the day as I wandered nearby Wollerau, another exclusive lakeside town where Roger spends time, and I wondered if I'd made a mistake trying to play tennis. Perhaps I'd need to learn how to play golf, as some had suggested to me.

I passed by a club called TC Kilchberg, where the greeting wasn't as warm as at Seeblick. I asked a couple who was playing on one of the courts if they minded if I took a photo of the club (since they'd be in it, albeit from a distance). The spandex-clad woman said, "No, you can't do that. You can find photos of the club on the internet."

The view looking down at the Einsiedeln Abbey, with its twin-spired, Baroque-style church and perfectly symmetrical courtyard from a steep hill dotted with horses and mooing cows above the complex, invites contemplation. It was here where Marc Dosch, who came to work at the abbey after becoming disaffected with the corporate rat race at Credit Suisse, outlined for me a thousand years of monastic life, along with some of his own story. Sitting on a bench above a hillside carpet of lush green grass, he pointed to an ancient chapel on the edge of the grounds, a disused Nordic ski jump, and some vineyards off in the distance, where the monks produce wine. It was so quiet, when we weren't talking all I could hear was the sound of the wind whistling across the valley and the clanging of cow bells.

View of Einsiedeln ©Dave Seminara

"I was burned out with my career, so I decided to come here for a one-year break," said Dosch, a tall, handsome man around my age with wispy black hair and a Roman nose. "But after a year I couldn't go back, so I'm still here."

Dosch told me that Benedictine monks believed in stability, so they didn't move from place to place like other Catholic orders. "When the monks arrive here, the idea is that this is where they will die," he said. Dosch wasn't present when Roger had his children baptized at the abbey, but he said that since the place was an important pilgrimage site, there weren't many baptisms held on site.

"But for someone famous like Roger, it's possible," he said.

After our chat, Marc ushered me into a stately room with high ceilings, creaky, wide-planked wooden floors, and many empty high-backed chairs where Abbot Federer greeted me like an old friend, radiating the sort of kindness befitting the abbot of a monastery founded by St. Meinrad, the patron saint of hospitality.

"Can I call you Father Federer?" I asked.

"Yes, of course," he said. "You know, before Roger became famous, I always used to have to spell my name. But now I can go anywhere in the world and they know the name Federer. Last year I was arriving at the airport in London, the guy at the border looked at my passport and said, "So where's your tennis rackets, Mister Federer?""

Abbot Federer, fifty-one, spoke English fluently. Like many Swiss Benedictine monks, he had spent time at Benedictine monasteries in North Dakota and Indiana. He said his branch of the family tree intersected with Roger's in the sixteenth century. Jakob's wife, Antonia Federer, was one of his relations—and Father

Federer confirmed that they came from the branch of the Federer clan that was expelled from Berneck after the great fire.

"Did Roger want you to baptize his kids because you're also a Federer?" I asked.

"I don't know. I think someone had told him that I was a Federer, but when he was here, I reminded him and it seemed like he had forgotten."

"Did you talk about ancestry, where your family trees crossed?"

"No, we didn't have much time together and I didn't want to spend the time we had on that," he said.

"So what did you ask him about?" I asked.

"I really just wanted to know what it was like to be him at this time in his life," he said.

I felt like it would have been an invasion of privacy to ask him what Roger said, but I did ask him if Roger seemed religious.

"I didn't think it was my place to ask him if he attends mass," he said. "I assume that he must be a person of faith if he's bringing his children here to be baptized, though."

I loved his open and trusting approach to religion, which is so different than some of the Catholic parishes I've been a part of, where priests want to give you the third degree and make you jump through a thousand hoops before performing sacraments on your children.

I asked Abbot Federer about how Roger is perceived in Switzerland, and he said that the Swiss aren't comfortable with hero worship. "Roger would be equivalent to something like the royal family in the UK, but here in Switzerland, we've never really had a super-famous star, so we don't know how to treat him," he said. "We are a very democratic country, so we don't really know how to revere people. Basically, we are proud of Roger, but we leave him alone."

I had brought a Roger Federer hat with the RF logo but had stopped wearing it after noticing that I had seen more of the hats on a recent trip to Colombia than in Switzerland. It almost felt the same as how only foreigners wear USA hats in America.

We prayed together and bonded over our mutual affection for his distant relation, and I accompanied him down to the church when the bells sounded signaling the start of vespers. Just before he ducked into the cathedral, this incredibly kind monk turned to me with a knowingly conspiratorial smile and said, "I really hope Djokovic doesn't win any more titles. I don't want him to catch Roger."

After vespers, an incredibly moving thirty minutes of sung prayers in the ornate baroque church, I was handed off to a young monk, Father Phillip, who was thirty-four, but with his red hair and rosy cheeks looked a decade younger. "I came here when I was twenty-one, and for years, I was the newest arrival, which means I

Einsiedeln Cathedral ©Dave Seminara

had the least seniority," he said. "Now there are others more junior than me, which is good." I was curious to know how one becomes an abbot. Father Federer was only fifty-one, so it wasn't like he had the most seniority. Was it just like any other profession where the most ambitious or hard-working or best-connected people rose to the top? I asked Philip a more diplomatic variation of this question, but I couldn't quite follow his response, which was, in essence, *well, it's complicated.*

Phillip gave me what amounted to a backstage tour of the church and the compound, which was magnificent, particularly the abbey's baroque library, which contains countless ancient scrolls and books.

"They called this the Dark Forest, not the Black Forest," Father Phillip explained, as I ambled about the library. "That's why the hermit, St. Meinrad came here in 835 and a monastic community was later founded here in 934. It's a quiet place, back then and also now."

He explained that according to the legend, Meinrad was murdered in 861 by two thieves whom he invited in and gave food to. (This is why he's considered the martyr of hospitality.) "You might have noticed that the logo of the abbey has two ravens? Well, the legend is that they were suspicious of the thieves, chased them back to Zürich and attacked them. The thieves were executed on a torture wheel back in Zürich. Now Meinrad's skull is on the altar of the church."

The abbey is famous for its black Madonna statue, and pilgrims come to visit Einsiedeln from around the world. Apparently the monks hid the statute of the black Madonna underground during the French Revolution, and later it was discovered in the closet of a Protestant family's home in Trieste. It was returned to the abbey in 1803 or 1804.

Einsiedeln library ©Dave Seminara

Father Phillip told me about the year he spent at their sister abbey in Indiana. "I liked it," he said. "Well, except for the food. They didn't serve us good food."

"What did they serve you?" I asked.

"Well it was like, how do you call, it wasn't full pieces of meat, it was like little pieces of beef, what do you call that?"

"Ground beef?"

"Yes, ground beef. It was always ground beef, never a decent piece of meat there."

What Kind of Fool would Prevent Roger Federer from Building a Tennis Court?

The only people out and about in Wollerau, a punishingly hilly lakefront tax haven just outside Zürich, on the Monday morning I visited in October were workers who were being paid to clean, service, or repair pricey residences overlooking Lake Zürich and the odd housewife ducking into a luxury vehicle. I found the address of Roger's former residence in Wollerau in the Swiss press. For a country that supposedly prizes privacy, it's surprisingly easy to figure these things out with a quick Google search. I took a train and a bus to the end of this street and then walked a good half-mile past mostly large, boxy homes, nearly all white or off-white, most with stellar views of the lake to the house in question.

The home was an anomaly on an otherwise pristine block. The lawn was unkempt, the garbage cans were overturned, and the place was in need of a paint job. A cat eyed me warily from the yard of this humble home, and I double-checked the article on my phone that had directed me to this unlikely place.

The author of the article insisted that Roger had sold this shabby-by-the-standards-of-this-fantastic-neighborhood home, but I assumed it had to be a mistake. Surely Roger would have something better than this fixer-upper? Had he purchased this home for his stringer or a masseuse, I wondered as I approached an older man across the street who was picking up his mail. He said his name was Uli; he was a retired textile executive and a big tennis fan who spoke perfect English.

"Roger and Mirka walked right by here one day a few years ago while I was trimming the hedges," he recounted. "I was excited

Home purchased by Roger ©Dave Seminara

because I thought they were going to be our new neighbors. But apparently there were some problems and they never moved in."

"What kind of problems?" I asked, my interest piqued.

"Well, they wanted to buy the property next door as well, knock them both down, put up a tennis court, and build one larger house. But the authorities wouldn't approve the zoning for a tennis court."

"Are you telling me that someone in Switzerland told Roger Federer he couldn't build a tennis court?" I asked, wondering if perhaps he was putting me on.

"No really, it's true," he insisted. "It's Switzerland, there are rules for everything and everyone. Aside from the court, some company outbid him on the neighboring property, so then he sold this house."

"So he never actually lived here?"

"No, never," he said, his brow furrowed as though he had just finished relaying a tragic story about someone who had had their head accidentally chopped off in a meat slicer.

Uli and I talked about Roger's chances of claiming his tenth Swiss Indoors later in the week; he was jealous I'd be at the tournament. He told me that Roger still owned another futuristic house—a much nicer one—just down the hill. He couldn't remember the street name, so I asked a municipal worker who was cutting down trees a few blocks away.

"Sure, Roger lives just down the hill," he said, offering me directions. "I saw him a few days ago, he walked right by here."

I felt like I was chasing a ghost. *You just missed him. Should have been here last week!* Another quick Google search confirmed the man's instructions. Home number two was on a block of modernist mansions, many built like layered sponge cakes spilling up the hillside, nearly all with epic views of Lake Zürich.

It was a bright, sunny, unseasonably warm day—the kind where it feels like a crime to be indoors—and I felt conspicuous walking down Roger's street for no good reason, guided by nothing more than curiosity. Roger's home was easy to spot—there were photos of it online—and there were several cars parked in front, including a modest sedan that looked like it belonged to a maid or nanny.

I paused briefly in front of the house to take a quick look and immediately regretted it after noticing a child's plastic truck on the terrace and a sign in Swiss German next to a staircase leading up to the house, which I assumed warned curious Federer fans to *keep the motherfuck out,* in the nicest possible Swiss way. I suddenly felt like a seedy voyeur—no better than the type who lurk near the entrances of peep-show booths, hoping to fulfill sleazy fantasies—and decided to beat a hasty retreat back up the hill.

As I walked purposefully up the street like a diner hustling out of a pancake house after leaving a stingy tip, I looked out over a canvas of homes, many slightly larger than neighboring Liechtenstein, and across the lake toward Zürich. A security van with some sort of insignia on it creeped up on me ever so slowly as I struggled to quickly gobble up the views. I had Rene Stauffer's Federer biography and an RF hat in my backpack along with the photo of the house on my phone. Oh no, I thought, I'm busted! A vision of myself being handcuffed and pushed into the van by a beefy thug, never to be heard from again, flashed across my brain. Did Roger have his own secret death squad for trespassers who poached onto his block?

Mercifully, the van kept going and my heart started beating again. I later typed the words on Roger's warning sign next to the steps leading up to his home into Google Translate and learned that it read, "Enter and walk the path at your own risk, any liability is rejected." The man thinks of everything.

In 2008, Roger bought a piece of land in Valbella (which translates to *beautiful valley* in English), near a popular ski resort in neighboring Lenzerheide, and proceeded to build a dream home and a connecting guesthouse for his parents that they moved into in 2012. Federer doesn't telegraph where he's staying at any given time, but apparently this has been the family's primary legal residence when they're in Switzerland for the last several years.

Federer could obviously live anywhere in the world. Hell, he could probably orbit the planet and live on a spaceship if he wanted to. If Roger wanted a ski house, why hadn't he relocated to the more famous resorts like Zermatt, Wengen, St. Moritz, or Davos? I had to see the Valbella/Lenzerheide area for myself, so I boarded a southbound train toward Chur on Monday afternoon, more than a little excited to be heading for the mountains.

The train was perhaps half full, but this being Switzerland, not a creature was stirring, and so I relished the silence as our train sliced its way through a deep valley past imposing clusters of peaks high atop both sides of the tracks.

I'm addicted to train travel, but the heartbreaking aspect of it is that you pass through places that look enticing and you feel the urge to get off and explore them. We passed a mountain village named Flums that had a stunning castle and a nice collection of Alpine-style homes and I wished that I had time to take a break from my Federer quest to check the place out. What goes on in Flums, Switzerland? I'll be damned if I know, but perhaps someday I'll find out.

I did make a pit stop in Sargans, flush against the Liechtenstein border, where Kenny Banzer, a friend who also happens to hold the distinction of being the youngest person to compete in the

Davis Cup, at fourteen, lives. I wrote a story about Kenny and a Togolese man who was the oldest to play Davis Cup, at sixty, for *The New York Times*, several years ago and we stayed in touch, in part because of our common affinity for Roger.

But Kenny and his wife had just had a baby, and so I couldn't convince him to come to Valbella with me. I showed him some of the photos from my Federer home tour excursions at his home in Vaduz, Liechtenstein's capital, and he laughed.

"I don't think Swiss people would do something like this," he said of my quest.

Liechtensteiners are a lot like their Swiss cousins when it comes to privacy and disdaining hero worship, and so Kenny had no interest in seeing Roger's neighborhoods even though he's a big Federer fan.

I took a bus from Chur, a charming mountain town of pedestrianized streets and quiet medieval squares, toward my hotel, the venerable Hotel Schweizerhof, a century old lodge in Lenzerheide, deep in the Swiss Alps in the canton of Graubünden.

The bus climbed south up countless switchbacks in the fading light around five in the evening past alpine splendor of Swiss postcard legend. There were church steeples with clock towers, impossibly green carpets of grass undulating across the hills and, of course, the kind of immensely pretty, almost regal cows that are so lovely they could compete in beauty contests if only they could fit into swimsuits and memorize vapid sound bites about saving the Amazon and fighting climate change.

The bus was exactly half full—commuters returning from their jobs sat in the window seats next to vacant aisle seats but no one except for me looked out the window at the splendid scenery. Everyone else was spending quality time basking in the warm glow of their phones and one could have heard a pin drop on the bus. I wanted to strike up a conversation with someone, ask them what the area was like, perhaps talk to them about Roger, but on a silent bus ride like this one, such an inquiry would have been akin to asking a stranger for a handjob. It just wasn't appropriate. My job was to remain silent, just like everyone else, but it felt lonely to just sit there watching my hapless American cellphone fail to load webpages.

Hotel Schweizerhof, my home in Lenzerheide for two nights, turned out to be a rambling, historic, and immensely likeable place situated in the heart of the village since 1904. Angela, a pretty young Swiss woman who told me she'd just returned from a stint working in a hotel in the UK, checked me in and then accompanied me up to and then inside my room to tell me more about the hotel. Ordinarily, I would have been eager to continue the conversation, but Roger's first-round match with Peter Gojowczyk, the big-serving German with far too many consecutive consonants in his name had just started and I wanted to tune in.

I had strategically planned my trip so that I'd arrive in Basel on Wednesday in the hopes of getting to see Roger play four times at the Swiss Indoors, assuming he made it to the final. Of course, I lived with the fear that Gojowczyk would win the damn match and ruin everything. The night before, I had woken in a cold sweat in the middle of the night after having a horrible nightmare involving Gojowczyk beating Roger.

In the dream, I was spared the match itself, but I walked into a bar and saw the German arms raised aloft in triumph, his beaky nose and perfectly coiffed blonde hair facing the heavens, on a TV screen above the bar. I frantically asked a number of patrons if the German journeyman had just beaten Federer, but none seemed to care. The bastards! *Roger lost and all of you fuckers are just sitting here enjoying your miserably overpriced beers?*

Luckily it was all a horrible dream. I woke up soaked in sweat and checked my phone to confirm that the match hadn't taken place yet. *Phew.*

Just as Angela was probably about halfway through her lengthy spiel about the hotel's Wi-Fi, breakfast procedures, the hotel's Turkish hammam and its variety of pools, and God knows what else, I curtly segued to Roger's match.

"Do you know what channel Roger's match is on?" I asked, grabbing the remote.

She gave me a quizzical look as though she didn't understand.

"Roger Federer," I stammered. "He's playing in Basel right now and…I'm sure the match must be on TV."

She had no idea. Members of the American tennis media often portray Switzerland as a country that hangs on Roger's every breath. But while he's obviously revered by many, I was beginning to realize that there are also quite a few people in Switzerland who don't give a damn about tennis or Roger Federer. Pity the poor ignorant Swiss fools living in their racquet-less homes oblivious to the tennis genius that lives amongst them.

Roger relieved my anxiety by dismantling the erratic German in fifty-three minutes, 6–2, 6–1, leaving me with plenty of time to soak in the hammam and explore the town. It was a cool, clear evening, great for stargazing, but a long walk down the village's main street past ski shops and banks and upscale boutiques, all closed, was depressing. October in a ski town—mud season—can be a dismal affair. At nine o'clock at night there wasn't a soul out and about; it was as if a nuclear bomb had struck Lenzerheide.

Lenzerheide ©Dave Seminara

I wondered what on earth Roger did if he wasn't in his home watching movies in his home cinema on a night like this. I read online that the Federers enjoy bringing their children to a Lego club at the Valbella Resort, designed by a Danish executive at Lego who has a home in the area. But surely that must get old. I considered checking out La Riva, which is reputedly their favorite restaurant, but thought better of it when I saw their criminally expensive menu, which features twenty-two pages of scandalously pricey wines and appetizers like cold cauliflower with almonds, figs, and mustard for $26. The vegetarian menu with wine costs $170, and the price goes up $100 more for carnivores. But surely Roger and Mirka saved money using the kid's menu for the twins, right? Well, a bit. The Paw Patrol Mini burger with fries costs $16, and schnitzels are $24. (If I was running a country, which thank goodness I'm not, anyone attempting to sell an item on a children's menu for $24 would be sent to a labor camp, it not worse.)

Perhaps he and Mirka came to my hotel to soak in the hammam, I wondered? I asked another young woman at the hotel when I returned if she'd ever seen them in the place. She smiled, indicating with her twinkling blue eyes that the answer was yes, but said, "Oh, I can't say. We don't talk about other guests."

Day Five

"You Will Shower in the Same Place Roger Showered"

fter my abbreviated tennis comeback attempt at TC See-blick, I was itching for a longer tryout, and hoped I might get one with Toni Poltera, a gregarious morning host for the Romansh-language radio service (Radiotelevisiun Svizra Rumantscha) of the Swiss Broadcasting Corporation. Toni is also the President of Tennisclub Felsberg, a small club in the area where Roger has prepared for the clay court season on several occasions.

Toni picked me up at the hotel promptly at 9:00 a.m. (they say that if you're not five minutes early in Switzerland, you're late, and it's no joke) on a perfect Indian Summer morning of blue skies and balmy temperatures. A square-jawed man with a neatly cropped haircut and fashionable glasses, he was wearing a blue button-down shirt with a "Polo Players Society" crest. A former decathlete, Toni appeared to be in his late forties or early fifties, and I loved his upbeat attitude.

"Thanks for coming to get me so early," I said.

"Early?" he said. "Nine is not early, I'm usually up at four."

Toni hosts a popular morning radio show and so the 9:00 a.m. start was like sleeping until noon for him. "How much time do you have?" I asked as we piled into his Volvo.

"All day if you want," he said with a smile. "It's my day off."

We drove south on a snaking country road past villages perched precariously on green hillsides below peaks that looked like they were created by a drunk child on an Etch A Sketch through the villages of Muldain and Lain, humble but lovely little places that (I later discovered) have no Wikipedia pages. Toni stopped at a ski lift and said, "Look they're making snow, even in this weather, you want to take a photo?"

I marveled at the scenery and Toni slowed down and proclaimed, "This is the same road Roger drives on, he loves these same views you are seeing. Seeing these views, breathing this fresh air, it gives you power!"

Toni told me that the canton we were touring—Grisons in French, Graubünden in German, Grigioni in Italian, and Grischun in Romansh, Toni's native tongue, the country's fourth official language—is one of the smallest cantons by population, but it has the largest land area. It's sort of the wild, wild east of Switzerland. According to news reports, Roger is apparently fond of the region because he grew up skiing in Lenzerheide.

We were listening to the Romansh-language morning show that Toni hosts five days per week. I loved the melodic tone of the language; it sounded to my ears more Italian than anything else. Toni grew up nearby and is one of some sixty thousand Romansh speakers in the country.

"Roger speaks so many languages, but does he know any Romansh?" I asked.

"Bah, I don't think so," Toni said.

He may be right, but I later read that the words *Tgesa Tgerigna*, which means "lovely house" in Romansh, are stenciled on Roger's Valbella home.

I asked Toni to teach me something in Romansh.

"*Grazia fitch*," he said. "That's 'thank you very much.'"

We zigzagged from one paved country road to another through frozen-in-time villages that were silent on this October Tuesday morning until Toni said, "I want to show you something; do you mind a bumpy unpaved road?"

Toni steered the car down onto a rough, narrow gravel road and we barreled through a forest for about a mile until we caught sight of a small, ancient church, St. Peter's, nestled in a valley below us.

"This is one of the oldest churches in Switzerland," Toni said, as we parked next to a ramshackle farmhouse beside the church. I looked it up later on and found out that the place was built

St. Peter's Church in Mistail ©Dave Seminara

around the time of Charlemagne, around 800 AD. The farmer who lived next door was nearly toothless, chickens and overfed, mutant-sized ducks roamed his property, and a puppy came over to us and nipped at our heels as a way of greeting.

The church was spartan, nearly empty inside, save for some faded icons that gave the place a haunting, timeless quality; free of modern accouterments, the visitor can experience the place just as people have for centuries. After taking a look inside the church, Toni led me to an enclosed area on the side of the church that was filled nearly floor to ceiling with the bones of priests and monks who had served at the church over the years. "What does that sign say next to the bones?" I asked.

"It says something like, 'Here we are, soon you'll be joining us.'"

"I wonder if Roger has been here?" I asked.

"It's a famous place, I'm sure he has," Toni said. When I looked the church up later on, I noticed that its TripAdvisor page had just fourteen reviews, none written by Roger or Mirka, but they probably don't spend a lot of time writing reviews—or if they do, perhaps they're not using obvious usernames like KingRoger20 or the like.

Our next stop was a remote little playground, tucked in a pretty valley with views of the sloping, snow-capped Alps in the distance. Toni said that Roger and Mirka like to take their twins to this place and it was easy to see why they liked it. "You see," Toni said, sweeping his right hand off toward a snow-capped peak in the distance, "here Roger can have peace and quiet, he can play with his kids like a normal person."

Roger's neighbors in Valbella had taken him to court and won when he tried to erect a playground on his property, impeding their view.

Roger's neighbors, who clearly cannot be tennis fans, also objected to a two-meter-high wire fence he erected and some tall trees he planted in the garden, presumably for privacy. But news reports suggested that he was able to keep those, as they were in the planning permits.

I told Toni that I found it funny that even the great Roger Federer could have petty squabbles with his neighbors, just like anyone else.

"The guy who sued him was a lawyer, I heard," Toni said. "What do you expect? These are rich people."

Turning north, we ventured into Valbella, a charming little community with a handful of local businesses and Alpine homes perched across a hillside with views of Lake Heidsee and nearby mountains. I never asked Toni to show me Roger's home, but he preempted a potential request as we pulled into the village, explaining, "Roger lives here for privacy, that's why we're *not* going to drive by his home."

Nevertheless, Toni wanted to give me a flavor of Roger's views, and so we drove up and down the hillside streets, passing a host of expensive-looking ski chalets. We parked the car on a hillside and Toni said, "Let's get out here so you can see what Roger sees when he looks out his windows." From this perch, we looked out over the lake and the snow-capped mountains in the distance. It was a view straight out of *The Sound of Music*, and it was easy to see how calming it would be for Roger to live in such a place.

We made another quick stop at a high-tech little playground Roger had built in the area, perhaps after his lawsuit saga, and then it was finally time for some tennis.

"Are you ready to play?" Toni asked, and off we went on the winding road north to Chur. Toni was taking me to see his club,

TC Felsberg, which is a half an hour down a zigzagging road on the outskirts of Chur, where he works.

"For me, this seems too far," I said on one hairpin turn. "If I was Roger, I would practice much closer to home."

Toni was having none of this.

"No, no, no," he began. "You're married, you have kids, so you can understand this. Of course you love your family, but isn't it nice to get out of the house?"

I nodded that indeed it was.

"Well, exactly," Toni said. "Roger is a man just like any other man. It's nice to get out of the house in the morning and go to work. This is his commute."

"Maybe so, but it doesn't seem like the most convenient place to live," I said.

"No, it is convenient, it's two and a half hours to Milan, an hour and a half to Zürich," he said. "And anyways, Roger likes to drive, so this is no problem."

We made a brief stop at a bustling club, Tennisclub Chur, which was full of players on a warm Tuesday afternoon. But it was on a busy road and you could hear the hum of traffic going by. "You see," Toni said, pointing to the scrum of players. "This place is too busy. Roger must have considered this place, but he didn't like it."

Our next port of call was Tennisclub Domat/Ems, another bustling club nearby that was full of players of varying skill levels, from promising juniors to geriatrics who were close to needing walkers. "This place is also much too busy for Roger, but I wanted you to see their murals," Toni explained.

Indeed, they did have a series of colorful tennis murals, including two depicting Roger, one kissing a trophy, and another with a Pinocchio-like nose, along with del Potro snarling, Hingis smiling, Stan Wawrinka holding a finger to his temple, Rafa,

©Dave Seminara

looking like an enraged, hungry bull, with wild eyebrows preparing for a backhand, and other tennis greats.

A few minutes later, we arrived at Toni's club, Tennisclub Felsberg, an out-of-the-way place with just three courts, two small dressing rooms and 150 members situated alongside the Rhine River. Toni had a key, and we had the quiet forty-year-old club all to ourselves.

"We're going to play on Roger's court," Toni said, pointing to a sign above court 1 labeling it "Roger Platz." The court next to Roger Platz is sarcastically named *gurkenplatz* after a cucumber, the German equivalent to badlands or a lemon. "If Djokovic or Nadal wanted to practice here, that's the court we would put them on," Toni said, a smile spreading across his face.

"So it's a bit of an insult to be put on the cucumber court?" I asked.

TC Felsberg ©Dave Seminara

"Exactly, who wants to play on the court next to Roger's court?"

"What did Roger say when you showed him the Roger Platz sign?" I asked.

"He said, 'Oh, great,'" Toni said with a shrug.

Toni led me inside the small clubhouse with a rudimentary kitchen, a barbeque, a coffee machine, a smashed racquet above the door, and photos of Roger and various players he has practiced with at the club, the Brit Dan Evans, the Serb Miomir Kecmanović, and some Swiss juniors among others.

"You know how meticulous Roger is?" Toni asked rhetorically before answering. "This year when he decided to play the clay court season, he got the balls they'd be using in Madrid so he could practice with them here. And I think he chose to practice here because we are at six hundred meters' altitude, almost the same as Madrid. Also, we resurface our courts every year, so they are good quality. You see, that's how meticulous this guy is."

"When he practices here, do you have many people trying to get in to watch?" I asked.

"No, well, some people hear about it and try to get in, but we only let club members come," he said. "We have a groundskeeper who was like our bouncer, keeping people out. But you know, Severin [Lüthi] told me that one of the clubs where Roger practiced once, the owner of the club called a local radio station to say that Roger was practicing there," he said.

"Oh no," I said. "Let me guess, Roger never played there again?"

"Exactly! Why would he do this? So stupid. For us, it is an honor for Roger to play here. We would never do this to him."

Toni relayed the incident with a grave expression, as though someone from the offending club had defecated in Roger's locker

©Toni Poltera

or asked his mom on a date, and I nodded thoughtfully, reliving the indignity of it all.

Toni led me over to a small, eight-by-eight room with a tiny shower with a little plastic curtain and a sink. "You'll get dressed and take your shower right here, just like Roger does when he's here."

I shanked several of my first shots—I was very rusty, I'm not used to red clay, and Toni hits a heavy, uncomfortable ball that bounces up high. But after a few minutes, I found a groove, hitting my groundstrokes with some of the old authority I had before morphea had attacked my feet and legs.

I could hear the gurgle of the flowing Rhine just a few feet away as we traded groundstrokes, and I felt inspired to be on Roger Platz, stomping around on the same chunks of red clay that King Roger has graced. My feet were swollen and red, but I couldn't feel them. I was almost in a blissful tennis trance as we mashed shots in the brilliant October sunshine.

"I like this!" Toni exclaimed after one long rally. "I would not want to play you when you're healthy."

At first, we were just sparring, feeling each other out, not really going for winners. But soon enough we were belting the ball, challenging each other, having a blast.

At one point as we were both drenched in sweat and like a pair of boxers entering the fifteenth round of a title fight, Toni shouted out, "You know we've been playing for two hours!" And all of a sudden I choked up, fighting back tears on Roger Platz as the reality hit me—I was back playing tennis again after all of the hell that I'd been through! Roger is an emotional guy, one who doesn't mind shedding tears, but I'm more of a stoic type, so I pulled myself together and got through it.

But even if I didn't let the tears flow, I felt so grateful to be back on a court again. It's so easy to take for granted one's ability to step onto a tennis court, or even take a walk without pain, for that matter. I grew up hearing the phrase, "tennis is a sport for a lifetime," but it never occurred to me that I'd lose the ability to play due to health issues. I had to be effectively expelled from tennis in order to understand how much the sport meant to me. And out on Roger Platz I felt so lucky, so grateful to be able to play again.

After well over two hours of tennis, I was drenched in sweat, my soaked underwear clung to me like a bad Tinder date, but I hadn't brought a towel or a change of underwear, though I did have a pair of pants and another shirt to change into.

"Don't worry, you can use that towel by the sink," Toni said, pointing to a small hand towel in the "Federer shower room" I was to use.

Dave Seminara ©Toni Poltera

The towel was rough, and it certainly wasn't clean; I feared that it had been there, unwashed, since the club opened in 1979. Nevertheless, I decided to shower and go commando, as it seemed preferable to keeping my sweaty clothes on, so I hopped into the Federer shower and then carefully dried myself off with the small hand towel, and then got changed.

"Where should I put this towel?" I asked Toni when I was done with it.

"It's fine, just put it back on the hook where you found it," he said.

I had a chuckle thinking that perhaps Roger might have the misfortune of using this terrible towel sometime if he washes his hands in this sink or forgets to bring his own clean towels for showering after practice. Poor Roger.

Toni, me, and my aching, beet-red feet repaired to a café in Lenzerheide, sitting outside in the late afternoon sunshine. Toni told me a bit about what he'd heard from one of the men who built the Federers' dream homes in Valbella.

"You know, in Switzerland, it's traditional to have a big party with the architects and builders when a home is completed," he said as his tall glass of beer arrived. "Roger came to this party and when he finally saw his new home, he broke down crying."

"Really?" I asked.

"Yes, you know he has owned homes before, but this was really the first home they designed with their vision. I think it really got to him. He could see all the fruits of his success."

We talked about Roger and when he might retire. Toni explained that in Switzerland, most Swiss think that Mirka is the boss of the relationship.

"When she says, 'it's enough' then I think that's when he'll stop," he said. "But for now, it seems like she enjoys the traveling lifestyle."

"Thank God for that," I said. "I don't even want to contemplate tennis with no Federer."

"Me neither," Toni said. "You know what Roger asked me after he was done training at the club this year?"

"What?"

"How much do I owe you for the coffees I drank this week? That's the kind of person he is."

"For Roger, We Would Wait All Night"

"**D**o you have to leave this morning?" asked Angela, my friend at the hotel front desk, when I came down for breakfast.

Indeed, it was Wednesday, which meant that I had to leave Lenzerheide in order to make Roger's second-round match with Radu Albot. My body ached from my tennis workout the day before, but I was fired up to finally see Roger in action at the Swiss Indoors in Basel. But it was a picture-perfect day, and I was torn between tennis and the Alpine scenery of the mountains. I hope someday to be reincarnated as a permanent guest of the Hotel Schweizerhof in Lenzerheide, but until that goes down, I had to settle up my bill and hand my key card over. My consolation prize was a fragrant sachet with the hotel logo on it.

"You can put it in your suitcase and remember us with it," Angela said.

Before leaving town, I had one last bit of unfinished business. I ambled over to Tennisclub Lenzerheide—it was so close to Roger's home that I felt certain he must practice there, despite Toni's assertion to the contrary. It was a lovely setting for a tennis club, tucked right off the village's main street and with stunning views of the mountains.

There were five outdoor clay courts but the nets were down; there was also one indoor hard court, which looked like an ideal place for Roger to play, given the privacy, but the place was locked and the lights were out.

I approached an Intersport sporting goods shop across the street from the club, and a cadaverously thin young man and his female colleague from the store were both outside smoking cigarettes, obviously not very busy on a Wednesday morning in October at nine o'clock.

The young man seemed to regard me cautiously and when I asked him if the club was closed for the season, he said, "Sorry if we seem a little nervous, it's just that you approach with dark sunglasses in the morning, and we saw on the security camera from last night that someone tried to break into the store. So we were a little worried."

"Oh, I'm sorry," I said. "I just wondered if the tennis club will be open at all today?"

"No, no, it's closed until the ski season starts," he said. "This time of year is very quiet near here."

I told them about my quest—like many others I had met, they had little interest in tennis or Roger. "Do you know if he practices over there?" I asked, gesturing toward the club.

"Sure he does," the young man said nonchalantly, as if it was a completely ordinary thing to have the best player in the history of tennis and a global sporting icon practicing in this small village.

"Too bad you can't get in because the owners of the club have lots of photos of him practicing there inside the club," he said, flicking a cigarette butt to the ground.

"Have you seen Roger just walking around the village?" I asked.

"I have," the woman said.

"What's it like, are people going up to him for autographs?"

"Not really," she said. "Not when I saw him. I don't think the Swiss really care very much about autographs."

Determined to see the evening's tennis program but still up for one last Alpine thrill, I took a detour on the way to Basel, venturing south to a village called Tiefencastel, where I picked up a Chur-bound train on the Albula line of the UNESCO World Heritage-recognized Rhaetian Railway. Built around the turn of the last century, various legs of the Rhaetian Railway connect Switzerland's famed ski resorts—Zermatt, St. Moritz and Davos—and offer a smorgasbord of jaw dropping scenery, countless bridges and tunnels, arched viaducts, sheer rock faces, idyllic mountain hamlets, and, of course, the mountains.

On this brilliant Wednesday morning, I was the only passenger in my train carriage. The trip lasted just under an hour and I was deliriously happy for every moment of it, as the train chugged past the century-old eleven-arched Solis Viaduct, ancient hillside churches, and remote sunlight valleys where pretty cows stood like sentries guarding their farms from intruders. Like the best sexual experience of a lifetime, it was one of those rides I didn't want to end. When we arrived in Chur, where I was to change trains for Basel, I resolved to return to Switzerland someday to do nothing more than ride its glorious trains.

I checked into my hotel, the Krafft, a trendy, bustling place on the Kleine (small) Basel side of the Rhine. The place was full of turtleneck-wearing hipsters in the lobby who looked like they could have played roles in *Saturday Night Live*'s old "Sprockets" show. I tossed my bags into my room, which had a sweet little terrace overlooking the Rhine, and took a tram to St. Jakobshalle, a modern eight-thousand-seat arena with two courts that's been the home of the Swiss Indoors since 1975.

The Swiss Indoors is an ATP 500 event that falls in a bit of a peculiar spot on the tennis calendar in October, when many of the world's top players are thinking more of the aimless offseason days spent ravaging their pretty spouses and girlfriends at luxury resorts in Mauritius than of winning tennis matches.

Nadal has played the tournament only four times in his career and Djokovic has played it just three times and has been AWOL since 2011. The tournament began in 1970, but until it became a Grand Prix event in 1977, when Björn Borg won it, it was essentially just a local tournament for good Swiss players.

Over the decades, a lot of great players have taken the title, including Borg, Lendl, Vilas, Edberg, John McEnroe, Becker, Courier, Djokovic, and Sampras among others. Entering the tournament, Roger had won the title more than anyone else, claiming it nine times. The arena is just a few miles from Roger's childhood home, his mother, Lynette, worked in the press credential office of the tournament for many years, and Roger was a ball boy at the event for two years in the early nineties, so it's obviously more than just an ordinary ATP 500 for the Federer family.

But as I picked up my press credentials and began to meet other members of the media in the press room, I eventually realized that I was the only native English-speaking member of the media accredited to the tournament. There was another ATP 500 event going on in Vienna that week; this, along with the high cost of travel to Switzerland and the absence of stars in the draw beyond Roger, Stefanos Tsitsipas, and Sascha Zverev meant that the reporters were all European, most from the region, which was fine by me.

Meeting other members of the tennis media fraternity can be a strange business. People size you up, judging you based on the prestige or lack thereof of the outlet on your badge. *The New York Times* has clout, but I felt self-conscious wearing the badge because people would say, "Oh cool, you work for *The New York Times?*" and I'd have to say, "Nah, I'm only a freelancer."

Low-key tournaments like the Swiss Indoors are much more liberal in handing out credentials compared to majors, and so there were quite a few young people who were essentially just tennis fans blogging for websites I'd never heard of who had never been paid to write a word in their lives. For example, there was a charming Japanese housewife, who was married to a Swiss man and lived nearby, who was credentialed to blog for a Japanese tennis website.

Some writers have a smug attitude toward these "rank amateurs," but I find that I tend to bond with them immediately. They love tennis and are there because *they want to be there.* On the other hand, in media centers at many tournaments, you often find a motley assortment of out-of-shape hacks, composing their stories from cubicles inside windowless bunkers without ever actually watching any live tennis.

The intimate arena was jam-packed for Roger's 7:00 p.m. match. The media center had no bathroom, so we had to queue up with the hordes. It took so long to piss that I took to avoiding liquids for the rest of the week, roaming the St. Jakobshalle arena dehydrated for much of the tournament.

The corridors of the arena were packed before and after big matches, but that was fine because the fans were among the best dressed and best smelling I have encountered at any sporting event in the world. Swiss tennis fans don't just show up at the tournament in a pair of jeans and a hoodie.

Nope, many of the men were dressed in suits or at least blazers or fashionable sweaters, and the women were dressed like they were going to an art opening or a dinner party. The total value of all the fashionable eyewear in the arena on its own would top the GDP of many developing countries.

I was surprised and delighted to discover that the prices at the arena's concession stands were simply expensive and not scandalously expensive, meaning that the prices were no higher inside the arena compared to anywhere else.

I wolfed down a bland but wonderfully colossal bowl of pasta at a high-top table just in time to see Roger walk on court to a rapturous greeting from the fans, who chanted and stomped their feet rhythmically as he waved to the crowd. The players were then subjected to pre-match interviews, which, let the record show, have never in sports history elicited an answer of any interest or value whatsoever.

The presenter asked Radu Albot, "How would you like to beat Roger?" in English. Albot, who wears his cap backwards and looks shorter than the 5'9" he claims, looked confused, almost as though he hadn't considered that he might win the match. He fidgeted for an awkward moment and asked to hear the question again. "Win against Roger?" Albot repeated, still looking baffled. Eventually he voiced some oft-repeated tennis platitudes about being aggressive and playing his game and the presenter nodded as though it was the first time he was hearing such wise insights.

(Tennis aside: I'm still waiting for the day when I hear a tennis commentator or player advocate for a more cautious or passive approach to the game. Why is it that everyone, seemingly no matter the circumstance, must be "more aggressive?")

Roger's lengthy intro was in Swiss German, but at the end of the long litany of his accomplishments the announcer lapsed into English, "Welcome home, Roger Federer!" to massive applause.

It was another unseasonably warm day and the arena was stifling hot, but most of the well-heeled-and-dressed fans were dressed for the season in sweaters and scarves, even though it was seventy degrees outside.

Even though Roger was at home, he kept speaking to himself on court in English (Come on! rather than *chum jetze*, which is the Swiss German equivalent) and played beautifully aggressive indoor tennis, racing out to a twenty-two-minute 6–0 bagel before Albot knew which hemisphere he was on. Up 6–0, 2–0 in what was quickly looking like a crucifixion, the hapless Moldovan finally held serve and celebrated the auspicious occasion by taking two deep bows facing each end of the court. He then pumped his fists emphatically and sarcastically, sending the crowd into hysterics. He lost the match decisively, 6–0, 6–3, but won some fans as well. It was over at 8:14 p.m. before I could fully grasp how excruciatingly uncomfortable our elementary-school-style plastic desks in the media section were.

Most of the assembled media scurried back to the media center, anticipating Roger's press conference. Tennis players sometimes hurry into their pressers if they're anxious to make a dinner reservation or another commitment, but sometimes they dally. In this case, Roger kept us waiting. And waiting, and waiting.

By 10:00 p.m. reporters were becoming irate. I commiserated with a gaggle of Italian-speaking Swiss TV journalists from the country's Ticino region.

"Where the hell is he!" one complained. "Our one-on-one with him will be the last one, too, it's always the German and French channels that get to go first."

The anticipation built to a fever pitch, and no one could go home until they'd sprinkled some Federer quotes in their already completed stories, which were in many cases 98 percent complete before the routine match was over.

Phillip, a reporter covering the match for a Zürich newspaper, told me, "For Roger, we would wait all night. Not for anyone else. He can do what he wants and there's nothing we can do." It was as though Roger was a tennis terrorist, holding us all hostage in the stuffy bowels of the arena in our media center prison. I heard a French reporter say, "He needs to get his fucking ass down here!" But there was no or else to his punchless threat. Of course, Roger was under no obligation to make our lives easy, and he knew it.

A host of pretty, fresh-faced college girls who worked as volunteers in the media center eagerly relayed updates to us as we sat in our cubicles and on sofas in the arena's humid belly. "Roger will be here in ten minutes…Roger is coming in five minutes…Roger will be down in two minutes," and so on.

The evening's second match—Taylor Fritz versus Alex de Minaur ended, and many of us grumbled, knowing we could have stayed in the arena to watch the whole contest, a win for de Minaur.

Right before Roger finally graced us with his presence, just after ten thirty, more than two hours after his match was over, the volunteers formed a double receiving/conga line for him to walk between, as though they were welcoming the Queen back to Buckingham Palace.

All the muttering and grumbling ceased as he walked into the room, wearing a blue hoodie with matching sweatpants, along with white sneakers, not his tennis ones, with no socks.

I've seen Roger in person before, but it's still a surreal experience to sit a few feet away from him. At once, it's hard not to be fascinated by his face, which is a marvel for cartoonists. He is oddly handsome—despite the prominent nose and the bushy eyebrows. His eyes, a brownish/green, are penetrating and intelligent, and he scanned the room, seemingly looking for familiar faces but also sizing us up before the questions commenced.

I was called on first, and he held eye contact with me throughout the question and answer. I asked him about some of his favorite tennis courts around the country to play on, hoping to elicit some valuable intel for my quest.

"They all don't exist anymore, so that's it," he said with a shrug. "They made real estate development on the one I grew up on and then the national tennis center in Écublens doesn't exist anymore...otherwise it would be the Old Boys club, and I haven't hit there in fifteen years. It just happens to be that way because I don't live in the area. But when I'm here, I visit my friends, my family, my sister, and everybody, so in terms of tennis, it's this court here, this is the special one."

Even though he effectively dodged the question, I felt oddly satisfied with the encounter because at least he showed me the respect of entertaining my question, pretending that it was important to him, holding eye contact, acknowledging my existence, treating me like a human being rather than a court jester in the presence of a king.

By the time I got back to my hotel it was nearly midnight, and a swarthy young man with exceedingly hairy knuckles at the front desk of the Krafft told me that there was only one place nearby still open that had good food.

"It's called the Star Grill, it's great if you like doner kebabs," he said as I began to salivate at the sound of those two beautiful words, *doner kebab,* which are often the best and only cheap meal you can find in Switzerland, particularly late at night. (I had already eaten about half a dozen of them so far in this trip.) "But you'll have to walk through the red-light district, and I don't know if you want to do that as it's kind of a little rough."

I almost laughed. Somehow the idea of Swiss hookers didn't really scare me, especially at this moment when I was desperate for food. But Basel's small red-light district was a lot sketchier than I imagined, and the working girls were more aggressive than what I imagine you'd find in Manila or Bangkok.

Most were from Africa or South Asia and had strong accents. They didn't just call out at me from a safe distance as one might expect in a red-light district. One by one they accosted me in the middle of the street, literally tugging at my clothing, pleading with me to join them for some late-night fun. I had to physically shake them off, the way one would try to brush off fleas, but as soon as I'd lose one, another would take her place.

"Come on, let's go, you have hotel, I make you so happy! It's not expensive, please mister."

I had never experienced anything quite like it—it was a quiet Wednesday night and I must have looked like a great potential customer, which didn't exactly fill me with self-confidence. It's never a good feeling to look like a classic John.

When I made it to the hole-in-the-wall kebab shop, it was filled with more prostitutes and their pimps, most nursing cups of tea complaining about business being slow, or so I imagined by their expressions. When my food came, I cringed as one of the working girls who had pursued me most aggressively took a seat on a stool next to me at the counter. I expected her to resume her sales pitch—come on, I show you good time—but instead she just gave me an apologetic smile and said, "Long night, huh?"

"The Charmest, Most Sympathetic, Most Interesting Sports Man in the World"

escribed by the Swiss tourism authority as Basel's miniature Versailles, the Villa Wenkenhof is an imposing place to approach on foot. Two giant golden deer stand like sentries in front of a twelve-foot-tall gate while the early-eighteenth-century chateau sits at the end of a long row of perfectly sculpted hedges that ooze wealth and privilege. I was at the gates promptly at 9:00 a.m. on a cool Thursday morning to meet Claudine Sommer, who promised to give me a tour of this magnificent country estate, just outside Basel in Riehen. It was here that Roger and Mirka wed on April 11, 2009, a few months before the birth of Myla Rose and Charlene Riva, their first set of twins.

Claudine explained that the estate's French-style gardens were open to the public every day but Saturday. Local officials

Villa Wenkenhof ©Dave Seminara

in Riehen sometimes offer tours of the interior of the estate, but it's generally closed. She said that an eccentric man with a large collection of typewriters has an office on the second floor but alas she couldn't take me up there.

A kind, petite woman of perhaps forty, she spoke with an endearing accent and seemed to be in a hurry to show me the estate's sparsely furnished rooms. "Zis is zee garden room, zis is where zey had dinner…zis is zee red room, here is where they had some lounge chairs—all zee antique furniture was removed for zee affair—zee music was here also."

The gardens were lovely, and Claudine was keen to show me the former horse stable, an oddly stately building with imposing pillars. "Zis is where zey made zer pictures," she said.

Claudine's job was to rent the place for weddings and other events, and she didn't know much about the history of the place, other than that it was opened in 1735.

"What was the wedding like?" I asked.

Villa Wenkenhof ©Dave Seminara

"I didn't work here at zis time, but I heard it was quite a small wedding," she said. "It was a secret."

"Do you get more bookings because people want to get married where Roger and Mirka married?" I asked.

"I don't sink so," she said. "There was some, how you call it, publicizing in zee papers, at zee time, but now I sink everyone has forgotten."

She said she didn't follow tennis, but she still liked Roger.

"Roger is zee charmest, most sympathetic, most interesting sports man in zee world, I think," she said before I said goodbye.

The joyful *thwack* of tennis balls filled the air the moment I stepped off the tram at the Bernerring stop just south of the city. Just steps away is the venerable Tennis Club Old Boys, where Roger honed his game from the age of eight until he moved to Écublens to train at the national tennis center at age fourteen. Founded in 1927, Old Boys is Basel's premier tennis club.

It was a bright and warm Thursday afternoon when I visited, and I was surprised that everyone was playing inside a bubble, rather than on the outdoors courts. Court 1 is named after Roger; court 2 for his childhood friend Marco Chiudinelli, who reached a career-high ranking of fifty-two in 2010 and retired in 2017.

By and large, tennis players lead privileged lives, so I don't want to pretend that Marco Chiudinelli's sad plight is akin to that of starving Somali refugees or triple amputees with leprosy, but let's face it, a guy like Marco must get *awfully tired* of fielding questions about his famous friend. *So, has he always been, like, a lot better than you? Did you know from an early age that he'd be famous and you'd be nothing more than an obscure journeyman whom no one outside a small circle of tennis players at the Old Boys Club in Basel and in the Swiss Federation cares about?* And so on and so forth. It's a miracle if Marco doesn't secretly despise Roger, even if he would never admit it. As the memorable Morrissey song goes, "We Hate It When Our Friends Become Successful." Oh, poor Marco, relegated to having court 2 named after him at his childhood club. And with that, I formally announce this lengthy Marco Chiudinelli pity-party paragraph officially over. Now back to the story.

In 2009, I conducted a lengthy telephone interview with one of Roger's first coaches, Madeleine Bärlocher, who was the director of the junior tennis program when Roger trained at the club, for a piece I was working on in *The New York Times*. Madeline agreed to meet me in the club's café, and I arrived twenty minutes early to

Tennis Club Old Boys ©Dave Seminara

Old Boys Club ©Dave Seminara

find her having lunch seated near a wall-size mural of Roger with the words, "Home of a Legend."

"Sit down with me," she said. "I hope you don't mind I'm having lunch. For twenty francs, you get a three-course lunch here with dessert, which is not bad for Basel."

Bärlocher, who is in her seventies but looks younger, told me that she had to stop teaching several years ago due to health challenges that left her with balance problems and other issues. She brought me a commemorative book about the club that was produced in 2002 for its seventy-five-year anniversary. She seemed a little sad and wistful, and I wondered if perhaps being back at the club reminded her that she was no longer fit enough to be on the court, a theme I could relate to.

But as we looked at some of the old photos of Roger in the book she lit up, reminiscing about the good old days. "Roger was always so competitive," she said, looking at a photo of him

Madeleine Bärlocher ©Dave Seminara

Roger Federer

Roger Federer als Schweizer Meister
Jun. Kat. IV 1991/92

Erfolgreiches IC-Team 1994 schaffte den Aufstieg
in der Nat. C
Hinten: Ph. Füglistaller, A. Müller, R. Gabrielli
Vorne: Ch. Wyss, S. S. Gabrielli, R. Federer
(T. Wimmer, fehlt)

Roger Federers Coup –
Tennismeister bei den 18jährige

An den nationalen Hallen-Tennismeisterschaften der Junioren in Luzern gewann der 15jähri
Roger Federer seinen ersten Titel in der U18-Alterskategorie ohne Satzverlust.

Roger Federer und Jon La Roche, 1993

Old Boys yearbook

beaming, holding what was perhaps his first trophy at age ten in 1991. "He hated to lose!"

When I interviewed Madeleine in 2009, she said, "After he'd lose a match, he'd sit under the umpire's chair and cry for half an hour sometimes. The other players would already be in the clubhouse eating sandwiches, and he'd still be crying on the court... Then he cried when he lost, now he cries when he wins."

Old Boys cafe ©Dave Seminara

I asked her about those comments and Roger's tendency to break down after emotional wins or losses. "It was right on that court over there," she said, gesturing toward court 1 to explain the incident she described to me in 2009. "I can remember it like it was yesterday, when I had to pull him off the court and explain to him that he wasn't the only person capable of playing good tennis."

Although she didn't say it, I sensed that in her generation crying and tennis didn't mix. *There's no crying in tennis!* Bärlocher explained that she had once been a promising player herself, having competed in Junior Wimbledon in 1958 after reaching the final of the junior national tournament that year. "The girl who beat me in the final had already been to Wimbledon before, so they said it was my turn," she said with a laugh. "Things were never easy for me because my father died when I was thirteen years old."

Old Boys ©Dave Seminara

When our conversation drifted back to Roger, I asked her if she recognized Federer's potential from an early age.

"I knew he was good, of course, but I never thought Roger would come so far and play so long," she said. "He acts the same now as he did when he was a boy here at the club, he likes to joke around now, just like then. He's the same person I knew then."

Although she hadn't seen Federer in many years, she could recall everything about his junior career—even the court number (5) where he used to have his lessons with his late coach, Peter Carter, at the club. I asked her about Seppli Kacovsky, a Czech national who was another of Roger's early coaches, and a pained expression came over her brow.

"He deserted his family, he just took off one day," she said. "No one knows why. No one has heard from him. He was a good coach, a very good coach, but he had a drinking problem, even when he was coaching here."

Bärlocher told me that she still watches all of Roger's matches on TV, but she had no plans to attend the Swiss Indoors. Roger had said at the press conference that he hadn't been back at Old Boys for fifteen years, even though it's only a couple miles from the courts. The tournament is on a fast indoor court and the club's courts are red clay. I could only imagine how many people with Federer connections—old coaches, old girlfriends, hairdressers, third cousins twice removed, dog walkers, dog catchers—wanted free tickets to the Swiss Indoors, and how could Roger give them out to everyone?

"So when Roger retires, who will you support?" I asked.

"No one," she said without missing a beat. "There'll never be another one like him. If you want to learn to play like Roger, forget it, you can't copy him."

I had some time to spare before the evening tennis session at St. Jakobshalle and was hoping to find the site where the Ciba tennis club once stood before it was bulldozed to make room for an apartment complex. The Ciba club was affiliated with Roger's dad's employer, Ciba-Geigy, a pharmaceutical company, and it was Roger's first club before Lynette decided to get him started in the junior program at Old Boys, which is a twenty-minute bike ride from their old family home.

The club was in Allschwil, a southwest suburb of Basel that sits flush on the French border, and I had been corresponding with Andy Werdenberg, the tennis pro at Tennis Club Allschwil, in the hopes that he might know where the old club was located. Andy promised to show me the place and tell me some stories, so I agreed to meet up with him while in Basel, but we hadn't set a date.

I sent him a text after saying goodbye to Madeleine and he replied that he'd pick me up at Old Boys in ten minutes. Andy's

Gmail icon shows a jogger in a tank-top running bib with curly brown, flowing shoulder length hair, so I was a little surprised when I hopped in his car and met a stocky man with short, gray hair who said he was sixty-five years old.

He seemed frantic…a bit harried. "We've got to run back to my store," he said in a twangy South African accent. "I've got a running and sports shop in Allschwil and business has been terrible. I just got a call from a woman who wants to buy some shoes, so we've got to run back there."

We were barreling across leafy suburban streets, where women pushed costly strollers and the screech of trams was louder than a '73 Ford Pinto with a bad brake job when Andy announced, "The Ciba club was right down that street there."

"Can we go down there?" I asked.

"Later we can," he said. "I've got to get back to the shop. It'll only take a minute."

We drove through Allschwil's main drag—it's a lovely small town with Alsatian-style half-timbered houses from the Middle Ages. The place is cute enough to be a pavilion at Epcot Center or to have its own page in a Rick Steves guidebook. Andy said that his family has been in the area for more than four hundred years, but he had gone to live in South Africa for a time, hence his endearing accent. He had left his shop, Andy's Sportlade, unlocked and the woman was trying on running sneakers when we got back. "Who's going to steal anything here?" he explained.

The exterior of the shop was adorned with signs from Basel's Carnival (Fasnacht), known as the three best days of the year locally.

Andy knew her, and as they got to talking, it became clear that the transaction might take some time, so I went for a twenty-minute

Andy's Sportslade ©Dave Seminara

walk around the village. When I returned the woman was wrapping up her purchase, but another man, an obese Austrian who looked a bit like a wild boar with flaring nostrils and earlobes stretched African village style, had come in to buy some pants to go paragliding. I wondered why someone would need a special pair of pants to go paragliding but didn't ask. Is it wise for morbidly obese people to go paragliding in the first place, I wondered?

I went for another long walk, only to come back and see that the Austrian was now sitting down next to the shoes in a folding chair, drinking a beer, listening to Andy's stories. Andy showed us a giant poster of himself he kept in the shop, apparently from the seventies, when he wore very short running shorts and had a huge mane of shaggy hair and a bushy mustache.

"It was sex, drugs, and rock and roll back then," he said with a smile. "Not many drugs, though." He told me that the photo was taken after his best half-marathon performance—one hour and eleven minutes, he claimed.

Andy started to lecture me about Trump—"that's some President you've got there"—when the fat Austrian came out of the dressing room with his new pants on. He was literally bursting out of them, but Andy reassured him that he looked great.

The Austrian then decided he wanted to try on some Lowa boots. I looked at my watch—we had returned to the store an hour and a half before and my patience was waning. I tried to talk about Roger, but Andy turned to Brexit. "They're absolute idiots," he said of those who voted to leave. "Uneducated people. What a mistake, I feel that honestly. This will be a catastrophe for their country."

I reminded him that his country wasn't in the EU and things had worked out pretty well for Switzerland. "That's different," he said, before pivoting to a rambling monologue that I couldn't follow. (Though in fairness to him, I made little effort to do so.)

Trying to focus him back to my task at hand, I asked him if Roger had practiced at his club.

"Roger has played at our club," he said. "He could take all five of our courts, but he never asked for any special favors. He's a normal guy. His mom was some beauty too!"

The Austrian bought the way-too-tight pair of pants and some boots and, when he left, I asked Andy if he could show me where the Ciba club had been, but he changed the subject and I told him that I wanted to head to the arena to catch Stefanos Tsitsipas's match. "There's a tram stop right up the street," he said.

I couldn't figure out if Andy actually knew where the Ciba club had been or not. Did he want to lecture an American about

Trump, was he lonely, or just a really nice guy who enjoys hanging out with Federer fans? I left not having a clue.

Thursday night's prime-time lineup at the Swiss Indoors featured two riveting three-setters. Tsitsipas overcame a game Ričardas Berankis in three close sets and then Stan Wawrinka beat Francis Tiafoe 7–5 in the third, showing some flashes of the old form that won him three majors not so long ago. The two embraced at the net, and Stan the Man proceeded to celebrate with gusto, exhorting each section of the excited crowd to cheer for him before firing balls into each section of the stands.

I was sitting in the media section with Giovanni and Franco, a pair of young Italians in their early twenties who were covering the tournament for Ubi Tennis, a website founded by Ubaldo Scanagatta, the dean of tennis writers at seventy with more than 130 majors under his belt.

(If you don't know Ubaldo, google him, he asks the most entertaining questions at press conferences. He once compared his sex life to Grigor Dimitrov's, and Novak Djokovic does a great impersonation of Ubaldo's signature *not too bad* line.)

They were unpaid volunteers trying to gain experience in sports writing and were eager to know how to contribute to publications like *The New York Times*. They were impressed that my credential said *The New York Times;* I wanted to tell them how hard it was to make a living as a freelance writer but I couldn't bring myself to do it, so instead we talked about the match. Stan's win set up an epic Friday night showdown with

Roger. The two Swiss masters were set to square off in Switzerland for the first time since Roger beat Stan at this same tournament in 2011.

"Roger versus Stan in Basel," Franco said. "This is going to be a classic!"

If There's a $48 Cheeseburger on the Menu, You Might Bump into Robert Federer and the Twins

I slept poorly at the Hotel Krafft Thursday night. It was hot for October, and there was no air conditioning in my room. I had a lovely little terrace overlooking the Rhine, but there was a constant flow of people on the promenade, so if I kept the door open to get a breeze, there was too much noise. My phone vibrated at 7:00 a.m.; it was a text from Kenny Banzer, which read, "Too bad there's no Roger-Stan match tonight," with an angry-face emoji.

I was still bleary eyed and had no idea what he was talking about, so I googled it and discovered that Stan had pulled out of the match, announcing in his post-match press conference (that

I didn't attend for fear that I'd have to brave the red-light district again if I wanted dinner) that he had sustained a back injury in the final game of the match and would pull out of the tournament.

I felt like I'd been punched in the gut. I love Stan, but the guy played amazing tennis at the end of the match. If he had sustained an injury why on earth was he jumping around and celebrating afterward with such exuberance? Perhaps he had sustained an injury firing balls up into the crowd but was too ashamed to admit it? I don't doubt that his back may have been bothering him, but to pull out of the match less than an hour after winning seemed about as lame as a Lionel Richie sweater.

He could have slept on it, gotten treatment Friday morning, taken some painkillers and waited to see if he was fit to play Roger. I couldn't help but think his career 3–23 record against Federer factored into his cowardly decision to pack it in for the season.

My adventure for the day was a day trip to Biel to see Switzerland's so-called House of Tennis, a gleaming national academy an hour south of Basel in the French-speaking part of Switzerland. The House of Tennis (HOT) opening in 1997, after Roger had been living and training in nearby Écublens for two years. The HOT—my acronym, not theirs—is where Roger and Mirka first met, though they didn't become a couple until the Sydney Olympics in 2000.

Mirka Vavrinec was the Swiss national champion in the under-eighteen group at fifteen, so she was a promising player in her own right at that time. She was nineteen and he was only sixteen. The age of consent in Switzerland is sixteen, but perhaps young Roger didn't make much of an impact on Mirka until they got together in Sydney three years later.

Born in Slovakia, Mirka moved to Kreuzlingen, a small town on Lake Constance in the country's northeast, at age two. Her father ran a jewelry store in a shopping arcade downtown, and at age nine, he took her to a tennis tournament in Germany where she met Martina Navratilova.

Martina thought she had an athletic figure and would make a good tennis player. At the time, Mirka was into ballet and wanted to be a ballerina, but Martina sent her a racquet and arranged for her to have a lesson, and the rest is history. Mirka's pro career lasted just four years; her best result was reaching the third round of the US Open in 2001. I take that back, her best result was, let's be honest, snagging Roger as her husband. If she hadn't been a tennis player, she probably never would have met him. In any event, I didn't have time to visit Kreuzlingen, so Biel would have to do. After all, this was a Footsteps of Federer story, but perhaps someone else can do a Footsteps of Mirka piece.

At the train station in Biel, I wasn't quite sure which bus would take me to the HOT, so I approached a tall young man with strawberry-blonde hair who had a large Wilson tennis bag slung over his shoulder and looked a bit like a skinnier version of a young Boris Becker. His name was Jonas Schaer and he was indeed headed there, so I followed him onto a bus. Jonas was nineteen, and he told me that he commuted more than an hour to train at the HOT three times per week. On this day, he was looking forward to playing in a tournament set to take place over the weekend. He hoped to turn pro but wasn't abandoning his studies. I asked him who his favorite player was, and he smiled.

"Roger, of course," he said. "He's the best."

The HOT is a sprawling facility with dozens of courts, including outdoor red clay and plenty of indoor hard courts, where all

Roger Federer Allee Swiss House of Tennis ©Dave Seminara

the action was on this Friday. The street alongside the center is named Roger Federer Allee, there's a mural of Roger at the front desk, and there are posters of him and Stan all around the gleaming facility, which is the nicest tennis center I've ever seen.

I was set to meet Yves Allegro, a former pro player who was Roger's friend and roommate when he trained at Biel. Allegro saw me sitting at a table in the club restaurant, Top Spin, and introduced himself.

I checked out the menu and pondered the game/set/match meal for eighteen francs, the King Roger burger, which has raclette cheese, or the Stan the Man burger, which has mozzarella and pesto. Apparently one of the perks of winning majors in Switzerland is that you get burgers named after you. But is it a coincidence that Roger's burger is 1 franc more expensive than Stan's? I think not, and in light of Stan's withdrawal from that evening's match, I think Stan's burger should have been on a clearance sale.

Now forty-one and serving as the Head of Swiss Tennis for the under-fourteen juniors, Yves was dressed in a Wilson sweatsuit and looked like he wasn't far removed from his playing days, when he reached a career high of number 32 on the doubles circuit and number 210 in singles. I told him about my quest, and he suggested I visited Tennisclub Horgen on the west side of Lake Zürich, mentioning that Roger likes to practice there.

I promised to check it out and remarked that I'd found surprisingly good food at most of the tennis clubs I'd eaten at.

"Every village in the country has a tennis club, so you can always find a place to play in Switzerland," he said. "Unfortunately, some of these clubs are in trouble, but you can usually get a good meal at tennis clubs in Switzerland—that's how clubs get members, you need to have good food and nice courts."

I asked Allegro about his association with the HOT first as a junior and now as a coach.

"I'm a federation guy," he said. "I was the first person to play on the courts here when it opened, on that court right over there. Now I work here, and I love it."

Yves may love his job, but he acknowledged that it was a tough one. He said that Roger had increased the popularity of the sport immeasurably.

"We were so fortunate to have not just Roger but then also Stan, who doesn't get enough credit," he said. "Remember, we're not a big country. To have two guys of that caliber is incredible, and now everyone keeps asking us, 'Do you have someone who will be the next Roger or the next Stan?'"

Outdoor courts at HOT ©Dave Seminara

And so, while Roger had done wonders for the popularity of tennis in Switzerland and around the world, he had also set the bar for achievement at an impossibly high level, one that Swiss juniors will no doubt struggle with.

Allegro said that they have some promising young players training in Biel but it's impossible to know how they'll progress, what ranking they'll achieve. But Allegro said that with thousands of talented players around the world now, the chances of producing a top-ten player are astronomically small. It's entirely possible that none of the Swiss juniors currently training at the HOT will ever reach the top fifty, let alone top ten.

I asked him about Jonas, and he said, "He's good but he's not here enough. He's still devoted to his schoolwork, which is smart but it's not easy to do both."

Will Jonas or any of the other promising Swiss juniors ever have a burger named after them? Only time will tell.

After watching Tsitsipas beat Filip Krajinović in three sets on Friday night, I was still feeling a little sorry for myself that there would be no Federer-Wawrinka match. As a small consolation, I decided to treat myself to a meal, or at least a snack if I could afford it, at the historic, five-star Hotel Les Trois Rois in central Basel along the Rhine.

I had read that Roger and other players stay at the Trois Rois during the tournament, and as I walked into the lobby and breathed in the chandelier-soaked, Old World whiff of European elegance, I could see why. Impeccably dressed men and women of a certain age—people who looked like they spent more money

Hotel Les Trois Rois ©Dave Seminara

Les Trois Rois staircase ©Dave Seminara

on handbags and wristwatches than I might on a car—mingled as staff members, dressed like they worked at Downton Abbey, catered to their every whim.

I felt like a pauper, wearing a pair of khakis, Birkenstocks, and a hoodie as I walked across the lobby. Out of the corner of my eye,

I saw an angelic-looking little girl who looked oddly familiar joy-fully bounding down a grand staircase with a banner advertising the hotel logo with the year it was founded, 1759. *Who was she?*

I froze for a moment, trying to place her and then a few sec-onds later, my suspicion that it was one of Roger's twins was confirmed, as her twin sister and Roger's dad, Robert, with his trademark bushy mustache and eyebrows, followed her down the staircase into the lobby.

I froze once more, torn between my desire to take a good look and my fear of getting thrown out for acting like a stalker. I had photos of Robert's childhood home on my phone and my RF hat in my bag. Perhaps I could tell Robert about my pilgrimage? He has a friendly face and by all accounts is a great guy. But was it appropriate?

Switzerland once again seemed like a very small country in that moment, and I was about to introduce myself before a sudden sense of Swiss reserve and decorum took over and I simply left them alone, pretending as though bumping into the Federer clan was absolutely routine. By this point in the trip, I wasn't surprised that no one attempted to take a photo or said a word to the Fed-erer clan as they made their way through the hotel. In fact, I was starting to really admire the Swiss for their good sense of decorum and taste.

Robert and the kids headed into the hotel's formal dining room and I wandered the hotel's opulent lobby, not wanting to follow right on their heels like a crazed stalker. After a few minutes, I approached the maître d' and asked for a table for one. The prices were extortionate, but I figured I could have a bowl of soup or some salad and a nice glass of Swiss ice water.

The man gave me a pitying look as though he was regarding a beggar with torn, ragged clothing lying in a gutter with a bottle of cheap booze in a paper bag.

"Do you have a reservation?" he sniffed, casting a 'well I doubt it' look at me.

"No," I said.

He clucked his tongue, indicating that this was an unfortunate situation indeed. "Well, perhaps you could sit in the bar."

I scored a table outside the bar with a view of the Rhine and the fourteenth-century Mittlere Brücke (Middle Bridge), where they used to toss witches and other condemned criminals into the river in the Middle Ages. The prices at the bar weren't much better than at the restaurant and the menu was mostly appetizers—snacks and the like. After passing on the King Roger and Stan the Man burgers for lunch, I decided to have a 48-franc ($48) raclette burger. The price was felonious, but I was in a fancy place and I wanted to know what a $48 cheeseburger tasted like.

A few minutes later, a greasy, gooey mess of a burger was delivered, and I had my answer. It was pretty damn good.

Day Nine

◇◇◇◇◇◇◇◇◇◇◇◇

Bigger Than Erasmus

ttracted by the prospect of being able to publish his books in a city filled with high-quality printers, Erasmus of Rotterdam moved to Basel in 1514. Perhaps best known for publishing the New Testament in Greek two years later, he lived for a time in a narrow home that's now a pharmacy museum depicting Basel's long history as a hub for the pharmaceutical industry. On semifinal Saturday morning, I took a fascinating walking tour with Helen Liebendörfer, a native Basler who has a doctorate in history. Inside Basel's thousand-year-old cathedral, where Erasmus is buried, I asked her if Roger had eclipsed the great man as Basel's most famous native son.

She laughed. "Maybe so," she said. "I think more people know his name than Erasmus around the world for sure."

I had been to Basel before and had walked every street of its charming Old Town on my own, but with Helen leading the way and telling stories, I felt like I discovered a new hidden city that isn't apparent to the casual visitor. There were stories lurking on seemingly every street. We ventured up and down many of Basel's charming alleyway staircases, including one that led us to 31 Ginger Street, the location of the irresistible Hoosesagg Museum, a shop-window sized museum which features a different themed collection of miniatures each month from community members who loan the museum everything from Eiffel towers to ceramic turtles.

Later we passed a fascinating alley in the Old Town called Elftausendjungfern-Gässlein, one I had passed by many times without a second glance. The alley, which means Eleven Thousand Virgins Lane in English, speaks to a cherished local legend about eleven thousand virgins, followers of St. Ursula, who arrived in town by boat in medieval times and were eventually martyred in Cologne. Helen explained the nuances of the legend to me and I didn't understand even 50 percent of it, but even so, it's hard not to get excited about eleven thousand virgins.

Helen gave me a nice overview of the city's Carnival (Fasnacht), which is called the three best days of the year. Basel is perhaps the only city in the world that's best experienced on a Monday at four o'clock in the morning. On the Monday after Ash Wednesday, nearly every Basler with a pulse turns up in the Old Town for Morgenstreich, when on the fourth chime of the bells at Basel's oldest church all the lights of the city are turned off, and costumed marching bands called cliques fire up a tune to signal the start of Basel's Fasnacht. The exhilarating seventy-two-hour Lenten Carnival illustrates an essential truth about this cosmopolitan riverside city of 170,000 that hugs Alsace and the Black Forest. Basel may be best known for Art Basel, the world's biggest art fair, for its museums and pharmaceutical companies, and, obviously, as the birthplace of Roger. But it is, above all, a city of traditions, none more cherished than Fasnacht.

Shots of Roger at Fasnacht in 2016

I'm not sure if Federer has ever publicly commented on Fasnacht, but in 2016, he tweeted some Fasnacht photos with the hashtags #Fasnacht and #Basel.

Though he posted no photos of himself at the event, others did. The fact that he doesn't mind turning up at an event like this along with the rest of the city tells you a lot about him and the country, and why he's happy to stay put.

There was so much to see in Basel that I decided to skip the first set of the first semifinal between Alex de Minaur and Reilly Opelka. I was stoked for the Federer-Tsitsipas match and didn't fancy the idea of spending more hours in the excruciatingly uncomfortable plastic media section school desk chairs watching (nearly) seven-foot-tall Opelka holding serve and blasting aces as predictably as male and female leads falling in love in a romantic comedy.

On the tram ride from the center out to the arena, a tall, attractive, young Mexican woman noticed the Swiss Indoors lanyard around my neck and asked if I knew if there were any tickets available for the match.

"I've always wanted to see Roger play in person, but I've only seen him on TV," she said, introducing herself as Ariane.

Ariane had 100 francs ($100) and wondered if she'd be able to get in. I knew the match was officially sold out, but I told her I'd ask around in the media center and send her a text if I heard of anyone with an extra ticket.

The arena was stifling hot once again and there was a fever pitch of excitement in the air. After two cakewalks and a walk-over, Roger was on deck and against a very good young player to boot. When I took my seat, de Minaur had already taken the first set, in a, surprise, surprise, tiebreaker and was up a break in the second set.

Often times in situations like these, tennis fans will cheer for the player who is losing in order to get more tennis. In this case, everyone, save for perhaps Opelka's coach and his girlfriend (if he has one), had seen enough and the crowd was firmly for the Aussie. Predictably, Opelka broke back and took the second set in yet another tiebreaker, eliciting audible groans in the media section and around the arena.

"Oh, that's just perfect, isn't it?" said an Italian TV journalist sitting in front of me. "Now we have at least another hour before Roger plays. *Basta! Basta!* [Enough! Enough!]"

The Opelka-de Minaur show had gone on too long; it was like watching an opening band play a three-hour set when you just wanted to see the headliner come on stage. The third set featured more riveting service holds and yet another tiebreaker, won by de Minaur. The players had two break points each in the two-hour-and-thirty-four-minute ordeal. If the future of tennis involves very large men with very big serves, then the post-Federer era could be very grim indeed for the sport.

When Fed finally came on court close to dinnertime, the crowd erupted and he burst out of the gates in fine form, gliding around the court, taking the ball early, coming into the net to finish points, schooling the young Greek on how to play fast court tennis.

It was especially satisfying because I had been listening to two female reporters, one from France, one from Italy, gushing over Stefanos during the warmup. "He's beautiful," said the Italian.

"I know, and he's so…what is the word for it," the French-woman said before coming up with, "sincere and honest."

I love Stefanos. It's hard not to admire a guy who comes from a real tennis family in a country that's not exactly a tennis power-house. I admire players who attack the net and have a one-handed backhand. And he is earnest, but he often sounds like he's stoned, or is it just confused, in interviews. Many women find him irre-sistible, it's true. His hair is too David Lee Roth for my tastes, but I guess that's part of his appeal.

I wouldn't know, but a couple minutes into the match, I got a text from Ariane. She hadn't been able to find a cheap ticket—they were going for two hundred francs and up outside—but she got lucky when someone exiting offered her their ticket. Was it Opel-ka's mother, I wondered?

"I'm so happy!" she texted with a smiley face emoji. "There was a guy going out and he gave me his ticket."

Fed's vintage form often elicited gasps from the crowd. On one occasion he barreled into net without a hint of caution and whipped a fierce, swinging forehand volley into the corner before deftly finishing the point with a delicate drop volley that landed just over the net. The crowd had been holding its collective breath, but once it was clear that Roger had the point won, gasps of admiration and disbelief erupted before the crowd burst into a huge round of applause. (We snobs in the press section avoid applause under the bogus pretext that we don't care who will win the match.)

It was magical stuff. Roger dismissed Tsitsipas in 78 minutes, 6–4, 6–4, and it wasn't as close as the scoreline indicated. Even though the crowd was 99.9 percent for Roger, the whole thing was like a sad case of premature ejaculation. Of course, we loved every moment of the match, but it was over way too soon after the excruciatingly long and boring opening match. Some Swiss fans had even taken to rooting, just a bit, for Tsitsipas near the end. But 78 minutes of vintage Federer is a hell of a lot better than 178 minutes of Big Man Tennis any day of the week, so I left the court feeling good if not completely sated.

On this evening, Roger kept us waiting in the media center for an hour as hungry reporters grumbled about missing dinner. He finally emerged clean-shaven and dressed impeccably in grey dress pants, a white oxford shirt, socks, and white tennis sneakers. He looked like he was on his way out to a fancy restaurant, and he probably was.

When they called for questions in English, mine was the only hand that went up. It was such a routine win that I decided to ask something a bit off the reservation, just to see how Roger would react.

"Are you familiar with the Rocky movies?" I asked from my perch in the front row, just a few steps from him.

"The Rocky movies?" he repeated, eyebrows raised, as though he was a bit circumspect about where I was going with the question. "Yeah, I've seen them."

"Tomorrow is the final, if you were going to take a pre-match jog the way Rocky would before a big fight, where would you go and would kids follow behind you the way they did with Rocky?"

Roger smiled and pondered my crazy question for a moment before responding. He was clearly in a great mood and didn't mind entertaining it. "I won't do that," he began. "They would leave me alone, I think. They have other things to do, but it would be along the Rhine or somewhere through the inner city. But I won't do it because I don't go on runs in the morning for a long, long time now. I used to do that as a junior because I was taught, waking up, being tough, going for a run, I remember it was my coach Peter Carter at the time, but I wouldn't do it and they would be like, 'Oh, is that Roger,' that's how they'd react."

Carlos, a Spanish reporter for a tennis website based in Spain who loves Roger and not his countryman Rafa Nadal, queried Roger in English since he didn't take questions in Spanish, and then the presser drifted into German and French. I don't speak either language, so I just sat there, gauging Roger's body language and his reaction to questions. A fly kept harassing him, buzzing around right near his eyes and nose. And it dawned on me that even if Swiss humans know not to bother Roger, insects have their own set of rules, even for the best tennis player in history.

Mirka Has Beautiful Teeth

$\mathcal{I}$ was sure that the man pacing on the platform of the Neue Welt tram stop in Münchenstein at 9:00 a.m. sharp on Sunday morning wasn't Daniel Altermatt, a city councilman who had offered to show me around the Basel suburb where Roger spent most of his childhood. He was wearing dark sunglasses, a black beret slightly askew, a sweater vest, and jeans. He looked too bohemian to be a city councilman in an upscale, buttoned-up Swiss suburb, but after eyeing each other on opposite sides of the platform for several minutes, he finally approached and asked if I was Dave Seminara.

"Is it okay if we go on foot?" he asked. "I like to take a nice walk on Sunday mornings."

Daniel has a PhD in physics and his portfolio in the city council is the Department of Civil Engineering and Works, so he brought a copy of the original plans for the small Wasserhaus development where Roger spent most of his childhood. Daniel had lived in Canada for many years but had a somewhat unusual,

Daniel Altermatt ©Dave Seminara

quite posh British accent that was hard to place. It was a bit of a cross between Carson, the butler on Downton Abbey, and perhaps John Cleese.

We walked through a park toward the street where Roger's home was and Daniel pointed out various landmarks, including the Münchenstein Gymnasium (locked), where Roger attended before leaving Basel for the national tennis academy in Écublens at fourteen.

"My son played football with him until he left town," Daniel said.

"Was Roger any good?" I asked.

"I think so," Daniel said. "But my sons were much more into table tennis."

I asked Daniel about the various places Roger has lived in the area.

"A hundred fifty years ago, there was nothing here," he said, sweeping his hand across the air. "In the 1920s, the area was built up for, let's say the lower middle class."

"Do you think Roger's family had money?" I asked.

"I'm not sure, but what they had I think they put into his tennis career," he said.

It's a solid area, mixed with apartment buildings, townhouses, and single-family homes, but it was quite middle class, not as upscale, upper-middle class as I had imagined. Robert and Lynette lived in the nearby suburb of Birsfelden when Roger was born. Daniel said it was more working class than Münchenstein. "There's nothing to see there, believe me," he said. The family later lived very briefly in Riehen before settling in Münchenstein. As an adult, Roger lived in Bottmingen with his parents and then in an apartment with Mirka in Oberwil, just west of Münchenstein.

"That's where the rich people live," Daniel said with a smile.

I had assumed that the street where Roger grew up (Wasserhaus) was a single street but there are actually a cluster of streets of identical townhouses, all named Wasserhaus. They looked neat and tidy but quite plain, and I wondered how much they would cost today.

"Eight to nine hundred thousand," Daniel said.

"And that's considered lower middle class?" I asked.

"It is around here, unfortunately," he said.

At the top of Roger's street, there's a small playground with a slide, a basketball hoop, and a teeter-totter. Oddly enough, there are hours posted (8:00 a.m. until noon, and then 2:00 until 8:00 p.m.) for when this tiny playground can be used. "That's Switzerland," Daniel said with a sigh. "They don't want the kids playing at odd hours."

Roger's childhood block ©Dave Seminara

Roger's street is narrow, and the townhomes are essentially identical, save for one outlier who placed a large ceramic cow in his tiny front garden. The street felt like it belonged in Manchester or Liverpool, and it seemed too small for an outsized personality like Roger. I found it difficult to imagine him living in the place, even as a boy.

The home where Roger lived had a bright red door and a table big enough for two in the small front garden area. I wondered if there was a garage door around back where Roger could have hit tennis balls as a boy, but it was impossible to tell.

We rounded the corner on to a street with a canopy of trees. "This is a nice street, that's why there was some talk about naming this street Roger Federer Allee," Daniel said. "Well some chap took it upon himself and just put the signs up here, 'Roger Federer Allee' but they kept disappearing." Now the street has no sign at all, which is odd for Switzerland.

Home where Roger once lived ©Dave Seminara

Daniel said that in 2012 the city council looked into the matter and determined that there was a regulation against naming anything after someone who is still alive. "We would have to kill him to get the street named after him now," he deadpanned. A year after my trip, a campaign to rename St. Jakobshalle Arena to Roger Federer Arena fell 1,800 signatures short of the three thousand required to force a vote on the matter. Local media said that he's unlikely to receive any such honors until after he dies.

From Roger's block, I could hear the sound of rushing water and I asked Daniel what it was. He led me to a street just behind Roger's, which is where the hydroelectric power plant Kraftwerk Neue Welt (New World) is located. There's a canal that Daniel said dates to the twelfth century and it feeds down into the Rhine. It's a very pleasant place with a few benches where you can sit and enjoy the sound of the rushing water, and I could imagine that young Roger must have enjoyed spending time here as a kid. Daniel pulled out his book, which was full of Post-it notes, and showed me that there was once an old house near the mill. "They called it a water house, that's what the street (*wasserhouse*, which means water house) is named after," Daniel said.

My feet were killing me, so we returned to the parking lot at Daniel's apartment complex to pick up his car for the rest of the tour.

Power plant behind Roger's childhood home ©Dave Seminara

We visited Old Münchenstein, a collection of several old buildings and the ruins of a twelfth-century castle. Like many towns in the States, most of the shops had long moved from the historical center of the town to the outskirts where people could easily drive and park, and so there wasn't much to see.

The sound of church bells filled the air and Daniel told me that it was mostly a Protestant area, so as Catholics, the Federer family would have been in the minority.

We visited a secondary school where Roger spent four years as a student. I was surprised that in such an orderly country the grass was overgrown. It was a boxy, 1960s-style building; the gates were open but there were signs warning against drinking, smoking, dog fouling, trespassing, and so on. "We don't keep the school yard locked, but we tell them how to behave," Daniel joked.

Ping-pong tables at Roger's childhood school ©Dave Seminara

It looked like an elementary school anywhere, save for the fact that it had two ping-pong courts in the front yard where young Roger must have engaged in many spirited matches with his classmates, no doubt getting into an argument or two.

We motored south in Daniel's car to Arlesheim, a seemingly much more upscale, lovely little town that seemed like a quaint, prosperous French country town. "The bishop's court was here so that's why they built this beautiful Baroque cathedral," Daniel said as we walked through the church square.

We had coffee sitting outside in a nice little café in the village center—it was another Indian Summer day—and Daniel told me a bit about his background. He was a Liberal Green Party member, which, given the beret, didn't surprise me much. He had once served in the canton's parliament, which is in session for a few weeks per year. "Next year, I'm going to run for mayor," he said.

"How are your chances?" I asked.

"Well we don't know who else will run yet but I think my chances are good," he said.

He started talking about climate change and I began daydreaming until I heard him say, "Fukushima, now that was helpful, that got people's attention."

I nodded dutifully as though I agreed that the Fukushima nuclear disaster was indeed a very helpful incident.

I told Daniel that there was one more place I wanted to visit in the area: Tennisclub Arlesheim. It was here that, according to Rene Stauffer's Federer biography, Roger played Marco Chiudenelli for the first time, at age eight, in the final of what the club calls The Bambino Cup. Daniel said he knew where the club was, but it seemed like he was driving in circles, so I offered to punch the club into Google Maps on my phone.

"No, no, no," he scoffed. "I've lived here for thirty-five years, I don't need Google to tell me where to go."

And yet, he kept venturing down one street after another struggling to find the place. Eventually, we stumbled across it, hidden down a dead-end street. As we pulled into the parking lot, it occurred to me that it would be a perfect place for Roger to practice if he lived closer.

"This place is absolutely hidden," Daniel said. "If you hadn't asked me to take you here, I don't think I would have ever come to this place."

Daniel, I have neglected to mention, like many Swiss I met, isn't a tennis player or fan. I struck up a conversation with a very friendly young woman who worked at the club and she confirmed that Roger had indeed played in the club's annual Bambino Cup.

"And we have a guy, Reto Schmidli, who is a member here," she said. "He beat Roger 6–0, 6–0, when he was a boy, he's very proud of that."

"I know Reto!" I exclaimed.

Indeed, I had interviewed Reto a decade before for a piece I wrote about how infrequently Roger gets bageled for *The New York Times*. In August 1991, Schmidli beat Roger when he was twelve and Roger was ten, 6–0, 6–0, and no one has ever double-bageled Fed since. Roger was asked about the memory once and in his charming way, said he "didn't think [he] played that badly." I contacted Reto before the trip several times and even followed him on Instagram, commenting on his photos to get his attention, but he ignored me. He was a cop, or at least he had been when I interviewed him in 2009. I wondered if perhaps he didn't like how the article turned out? Here's how the story began:

There may be only one tennis player in the world who wishes he had taken it a bit easier on Roger Federer. Reto Schmidli, 31, a police officer and part-time psychology student in Arlesheim, Switzerland, is the only person who has "double-bageled" Federer, that is, beaten him, 6–0, 6–0.

The fact that the drubbing occurred in Federer's first tournament match, when he was just 10 years old, is not lost on Schmidli.

"I was just thinking about winning the match," remembered Schmidli, who is now a recreational player ranked No. 715 in Switzerland. "I wasn't thinking about being nice to him, but if I had to do it over again, I should have given Roger a game."

The beating took place at the Grüssenhölzli tennis center in Pratteln, Switzerland, in August 1991. Federer was scheduled to compete in the 10-and-under tournament, but there weren't enough entrants, so he was forced to square off against Schmidli, who was nearly 13. Schmidli had a significant size advantage and quickly overpowered Federer without dropping a game.

The match remains memorable for Federer. After notching a 6–0, 6–0 victory over Gastón Gaudio in Shanghai in November 2005, he was asked if he had ever blanked an opponent before. "No, but I lost, 6–0, 6–0, in juniors once," he told reporters, adding, "I didn't think I played that badly." Federer later told Chris Bowers of the BBC: "I actually played pretty good. I lost, 6–0, 6–0. I left the court and I wasn't even disappointed."

The woman told me, "If you like Roger, you really should meet Rudy," and pointed to a gentleman who was coming off the court with another man, both perhaps in their sixties. As it turned out, Rudy and Daniel had been classmates many years ago and hadn't seen each other since. After they caught up, Rudy told me that he and his tennis partner, Peter, were both dentists.

"I probably shouldn't tell you this, but Roger was my patient," he said. "I saw Mirka once too. She has perfect teeth, just beautiful!"

Daniel drove me to St. Jakobshalle, where I quickly bumped into Marc Dosch, who was there for the final with Abbot Federer. "I lost the Abbot," he said, and I wondered if perhaps he was in the locker room, giving Roger a pre-match blessing.

In his pointless pre-match on-court interview, Alex de Minaur was asked, "Do you think your fast legs will help you today against Roger?" He smiled awkwardly and said, "They better be fast today."

Roger looked resplendent in the Swiss colors—red bandana and shirt with crisp white shorts. Minutes into the match, Roger prevailed in a thrilling thirty-some-odd-shot rally—mostly backhand to backhand with each player pushing the other further and further off the court. During the point, there was also an exchange in the crowd, as some gasped while others angrily *shushed* them. A point later, Roger broke serve to go up 2–0 and the place erupted.

Up 5–2, women with angelic voices sung, very softly at first, *Allez, Allez, Allez, Allez, Allez Roger, Allez Roger, Allez Roger, Allez.* With each stanza their voices grew louder and more insistent. Frederick, a Swiss reporter sitting to my right, laughed. "Do you know this group?" he asked me.

I admitted that I didn't.

"It's one of Roger's fan groups," he said. "He met with them the Sunday before the tournament started. I wrote an article about one of them. She has been to something like three hundred of Roger's matches around the world. They are mostly lonely, sad women in their fifties and sixties who are obsessed with Roger."

I guess he assumed I was a reporter and not a fan. I wanted to tell him that there are much worse things to be obsessed with than Roger, but I was so delighted with Federer's level of play that I didn't want to take my eyes off the match.

Roger took the first set in thirty-four minutes 6–2, and it was pretty clear early on that he wasn't going to be denied his tenth Swiss Indoors title on this day. I could tell that many of the reporters around me who were tapping away at laptops were already about 90 percent done with their stories. One reporter from Agence France-Presse—seated in front of me in the front row of the media section, reserved for elite media outlets—was googling and then looking at images of *Fraggle Rock* as Roger began to coast in the second set.

I couldn't be sure, but my bet was that he thought de Minaur resembled one of the Fraggle Rock characters, though I wasn't sure which one. For me, the most troubling part of de Minaur's appearance was his stumpy mustache, which was way too close to Hitler territory for my tastes.

After Roger sent a looping forehand passing shot down the line to break de Minaur's serve to go up 2–0 in the second set, Roger's fan club choir sang, "Roger Federer, forever our number one!"

"Those are probably the only words they know in English," Frederick said.

The second set was a mirror image of the first, brilliant attacking tennis from Federer and plenty of what David Foster Wallace once called "Federer moments," occasions where Roger did things on the court that only Roger can do. There were two service breaks; it was another thirty-four-minute 6–2 set. Sixty-eight minutes and it was over all too quickly. Federer was like a brilliant meteor on this day; if you were too busy looking at *Fraggle Rock* images online, you missed him winning his tenth Swiss Indoors title.

A woman came out with two big numbers—a *1* and a *0* that looked like birthday candles—and then the ball kids started an exhilarating processional march around the court, swirling from opposite directions into two neat lines in a scene that was reminiscent of a spectacle from North Korea's Arirang Mass Games.

They played the Pomp and Circumstance graduation march song over the loudspeakers as half the ball kids got handshakes and medals from Roger, while the other half got them from Alex. It felt like a high-school graduation ceremony and, with all due respect to Alex, I could only imagine how disappointed the kids who ended up in his line were. Having served as a ball boy for two years in Basel, it must have been an emotional moment for Roger to place the medals on the kids' shoulders once more in his hometown. When Michael Stich placed the same medal around Roger's shoulders in 1993, he couldn't have known that that boy would become the greatest player in the history of the sport.

Roger got his trophy plus another bizarre one shaped like a hand. I could only guess that he must have been given a hand trophy after winning five Swiss Indoors titles and this was the second hand for getting ten.

De Minaur began his concession speech and, oddly enough, the PA system continued to play the *Pirates of the Caribbean* theme music. Between the music and his Nazi mustache, I struggled to listen to his speech.

Roger spoke in Swiss German, so I had to rely upon Frederick to interpret for me. A minute or so into the speech, Federer broke down in tears.

Normally, you don't want to see someone you love crying. But with Roger, I always enjoy watching him have a good cry. In fact, I love it. Perhaps it's because when he breaks down in tears, it's a reminder that despite his talent, fame, and wealth, he's human just like all of us. Or perhaps it's because when he cries, he allows us to join him in victory or defeat; it reminds us how much the sport means to him. Sometimes fans wonder if they care more about the game than the athlete they revere, but with Roger we know this isn't the case.

As I walked through the press center after the match, a tall man holding a camera stopped me.

"Excuse me, are you Dave Seminara?"

I always feel like I'm trouble when someone asks me this question, and this was the second time I was fielding it on this day, but I admitted that I was.

"You met my son Jonas on Friday at the House of Tennis," he said. I had forgotten that I had given the boy my business card.

"Oh yes," I said. "Wait, he didn't tell me his father was covering the tournament."

"He didn't? Oh well, he said he told you about the tournament he was playing in this weekend. I wanted to tell you that he won the tournament!" Once again, Switzerland was proving to be a very small country. Who knows, perhaps Jonas Schaer will be the next Roger Federer and I can claim that I discovered him. (For the moment, his ITF singles ranking is 1,797.)

After following the local tradition of treating the ball kids to pizza, Roger walked through the pressroom carrying his giant silver trophy. The press minders had warned us in scolding tones before he came out not to photograph him or ask him for autographs, and as he made his way past us holding his prize, it seemed like a cruel and unusual punishment to be prevented from photographing the moment.

Unlike the previous rounds, he was still in his tennis kit, unshowered, and it looked like he'd literally won the tournament without breaking a sweat. He had spent a total of just over four hours on court for the entire tournament, which was nearly an hour less than his 2019 Wimbledon final against Novak Djokovic.

As we sat waiting for the press conference to begin, I leafed through the Old Boys book Madeleine Bärlocher had given me and studied a photo of Roger hoisting a trophy at age ten. His expression looked the same then as it did on this day.

I sat in the front row, next to the Fraggle Rock reporter, and was once again called on first. I showed Roger the photo and asked him if the feeling of lifting trophies had changed over the years.

"It's similar," he said, eyeing the photo from a few feet away. "Has the feeling changed? Back in the day when you lift a trophy as a junior, it was like 'Ah, let's pretend to be one of the big guys' but you clearly know you're not. Now when you're able to do it in a stadium with people chanting your name or celebrating you or your tennis, it's a wonderful feeling. There you probably just had a couple of parents around and a photographer you know who happened to be there at that time. Luckily there was a photographer there because it was more of a luxury to have a camera at that time. So clearly things have changed. No, look, it was an incredible journey, it definitely hit me hard being here in Basel, I don't take these tournament victories as a normal thing, I take it as something quite unique and special even though it's been a lot by now, every one has a different flavor and I try to enjoy it as much in the moment as well."

Carlos was the only other reporter to ask a question in English, so I got a chance to ask another question and this time I ventured a bit deeper into very personal, non-Swiss territory, asking him what had triggered the tears on the court.

Roger answered my question very thoughtfully and directly, crediting his family and the crowd.

"I think it might be partially reminiscing about everything that went on this week," he said. "Also, definitely the family. The thought of the team aspect, the family aspect, everything that goes into me being able to do this today. People think you just go out there and just do it, and have these types of weeks, these types of matches at will. But there's so much more that goes into it, let alone managing four children is a challenge but a good one. So when I stand there and look back at everything I had to go through, it really touches me...the music, the ball kids running in already gets me going, and then, I think back to thanking the fans at the very end, which I know I'm going to save for the end, especially here in Basel and other places that are incredibly special to me. It leaves a mark for me and sometimes when it comes up and I know it could but I'm not sure if it will. It also depends on the applause of the people, how warm it is, how much they feel that I'm struggling or not, and how much love I get."

Imagine that, even the great Roger Federer is still impacted by the outpouring of love he gets from his fans. I felt like Federer's responses to my questions got better as the week went on and, though I had a press credential, I wanted to give him a hug or at least a high five afterwards, perhaps tell him about my journey. I couldn't do it, but I walked out of St. Jakobshalle feeling like I'd entered into a state of Grace after having an audience with the Pope.

I'd be a Federer fan even if I hadn't experienced the health problems that have kept me off the courts for years at a time. But when you're deprived of playing a sport that means so much to you, watching it on television can help fill the void. Prior to 2004 when my health first started to falter, I watched plenty of tennis, but there was no Tennis Channel (until 2003), I had no DVR, and I spent more time playing the sport than watching it on television.

Going to Switzerland to travel in Roger's footsteps and starting a comeback of my own also helped me realize that becoming a Federer superfan had filled a void in my life. When I couldn't play tennis, I could at least cheer for Roger, and that was important. But now that I'm (hopefully) on the road to recovery, that doesn't mean Federer and his matches will be any less meaningful to me. Now that he's in the twilight of his career, I'm especially cognizant that he won't be around forever, and I'm savoring every one of his matches like a man on death row might his last pizza, because Roger's playing days are sadly numbered.

As I waited for the tram back to my hotel, it started to rain, and my glasses filled with raindrops until I remembered that I had my RF hat buried in my bag. I hadn't worn it in more than a week in a strange bid to "fit in" in Switzerland. But now it was time to put my Roger Federer hat on and return home, a tennis player once more.

Epilogue

Roger didn't seem like himself at the 2020 Australian Open. He made it to the semifinals before bowing out in straight sets to Novak Djokovic, but Roger's level was far from what it had been for most of 2019. Novak went on to win the tournament, inching closer to Roger's twenty majors with his seventeenth. Djokovic beat Thiem in the final and the crowd was mostly against him. I felt like many are just like Abbot Federer and me; they don't want Novak creeping up so close to his record.

Djokovic's dad, Srdjan, added insult to injury in the weeks after the match, giving a series of inflammatory interviews with the Serbian press. In the first interview, he lashed out at the Australian crowd for rooting for "some Austrian" in the final. He also said that Novak would tie Roger's record *this year*. "This year he will equal Federer's [all-time Grand Slam] record because he will win all the remaining three Grand Slams," Srdjan Djokovic said.

"I think it will be October when he will catch him for weeks at world number one, too."

A week or so later, Srdjan stooped even lower, telling a Serb news outlet that Roger was jealous of his son, while also questioning Roger's "humanity." "Federer is a great tennis player, but that could not be said when it comes to his humanity," he said. "He is jealous of Novak from the moment he shows up because he knew he was better than him and would overcome him."

These are absurd comments that Novak would never endorse. It's actually unfair to compare Novak, Rafa—who equaled Federer's mark of twenty majors in September—or any other current player to Federer because he's one of a kind. Will Novak and Nadal blow past Roger's haul of twenty majors? Quite possibly.

Is Novak about to pass Roger's records (majors plus weeks at number one)? Perhaps so, but it won't change how I feel about Federer. And I don't think Roger is done winning majors in any case.

But I knew something was wrong Down Under when Roger had to save match points to beat John Millman and Tennys Sandgren, players who, let's be honest, have no business beating Fed. (Yes, I know Millman beat him at the US Open, but those were extreme conditions, so I'm calling that a fluke.)

Something was off, but I had no idea what until a few weeks later, when Roger announced that he was having arthroscopic surgery on his right knee and would be out until Wimbledon. It was a gut punch. Tennis without Roger isn't quite the same. But a few weeks after Roger's announcement, the coronavirus spread from China across the planet and the ATP Tour suspended its season for several months. As of this writing, Federer plans to return to the tour at the 2021 Australian Open. Let's hope that by the time you read this book, he'll have already won the tournament.

Being deprived of pro tennis had me wanting to get back on the court myself, but I've had my own injury issues to contend with. When I returned from Switzerland, I joined a tennis club near my home and started playing in a regular Thursday night men's drill.

It was fun—I wasn't moving well, but I was on the court smacking balls around with authority and it felt great to be back. Within a few weeks of joining the club, I was even getting offers from guys who wanted me to be their doubles partner.

I was back! But then all of a sudden, I wasn't. One evening, while stretching for a shot on one of the club's green clay courts, I felt a sharp pain on the outside of my left knee—the same one I had surgery on in 2014, and knew I was in trouble.

I didn't play for a month while I was waiting to get an MRI, which revealed no tears but a significant lateral arthritis problem.

"So, does this mean I can play tennis again?" I asked.

"You can," the doctor said. "Your ACL looks solid, but it might be painful, that's your only problem."

I returned to the sport slowly at first—mostly playing alongside my sons with my RF hat on against a ball machine, the perfect opponent in coronavirus times. But as our stay-at-home orders began to drive all of us insane, I found that my local tennis club was a refuge, a safe place that remained open where we could take out some of our COVID-19 frustrations on tennis balls.

I settled into a routine of playing with my sons and the ball machine every single day, something I haven't done in more than twenty years. It was a peculiar time to dive so deeply back into tennis, but I found myself with plenty of time on my hands and with nowhere else to go.

Because I'm on three immunity-suppressing medications, some told me that I should stay at home. And I did, save for my tennis habit. But I wasn't encountering anyone new at the club, just my sons.

At the beginning of the crisis, I listened to the audiobook edition of Gerald Marzorati's *Late to the Ball: A Journey into Tennis and Aging*, which chronicles a magazine editor who took up tennis in his sixties and became obsessed. Marzorati studied Federer's one-hand topspin backhand on video and tried to emulate it, and I was inspired to do the same.

It felt awkward at first—I've played with a two-hand topspin backhand for more than forty years along with a one-hand slice. But I had my sons videotape my efforts and it became a great project trying to get my swing to look Federer-esque.

I haven't succeeded yet, and I probably never will. But I've found the inspiration to dive headlong back into the sport I fell in love with as a boy and it feels magnificent.

Right after I re-injured my knee, I feared that perhaps my Swiss trip was my last hurrah in tennis. But now I feel like if Roger can keep going, I will too.

Federer Family Milestones
in Switzerland

1946   Robert Federer was born in Berneck, the son of Benedikt Anton Federer, a textile worker, and Katharina Federer, a housewife.

1966   Robert trained as a lab technician in the now closed Viscosuisse factory in nearby Widnau, where his dad was a shift worker producing synthetic fiber, and later moved to Basel.

1970   Robert moved to South Africa, where he met Lynette Durand, then an eighteen-year-old secretary in the company cafeteria. Robert, who had played soccer/football for FC Widnau for a time, took up tennis at twenty-four, and so did Lynette.

1973	Robert and Lynette moved to Riehen, just outside Basel. They would later move to nearby München-stein, where Roger grew up.
1979	Roger's sister, Diana, was born.
1980	Two-year-old Mirka Vavrinec and her family moved from Bojnice, in the Slovakian part of Czechoslova-kia, to the Swiss border city of Kreuzlingen on Lake Constance. Her father, Miroslav, a former javelin thrower, and his wife, Drahomira, operated a jew-elry shop in a shopping arcade downtown.
1981	Roger was born on August 8 at University Hospital of Basel.
1980s	Roger learned to play tennis at the now-bulldozed Ciba club in Allschwil, a charming suburb of Basel.
1986–1994	Roger was a student at Schulhaus Neuewelt in Münchenstein. He later attended the Progyman-sium Münchenstein for two years before devoting himself to tennis.
1989	Roger, then eight, lost to his friend Marco Chiudi-nelli in the final of the "Bambino Cup" at Tennis-club Arlesheim, which still hosts the event each year. Both shed tears during the match.

1990	Lynette enrolled Roger in the junior tennis program at Tennis Club Old Boys, a venerable club founded in 1927.
1991	Roger got double bageled (6–0, 6–0) in his first tournament match by Reto Schmidli, who was two years older at the time. The match took place at the now-defunct Grüssenhölzli tennis center in Pratteln, Switzerland.
1993	Roger won his first national title, besting Chiudinelli in the final of the twelve-and-under draw of the Lucerne Open. Roger participated as a ball boy at the Swiss Indoors tournament; Michael Stich placed a medal around his neck after the final.
1994	Roger moved to Écublens, in the French-speaking section of Switzerland, to train at the National Tennis Center. He attended La Planta secondary school.
1995	Lynette Federer won a (tennis) national championship in the over-thirty division as a member of Tennis Club Old Boys.

1997   Roger completed the mandatory nine years of schooling and decided to halt his studies and focus solely on tennis.

Roger moved from Écublens to Biel, as the Swiss Tennis Federation opened a new state of the art "House of Tennis" training center in Biel. This is where he first met Mirka, who was also training there. Roger moved into an apartment near the center with Yves Allegro, then nineteen.

Robert Federer received an offer for a job transfer to Australia this year as well; he seriously considered it but decided to stay in Switzerland.

1998   Roger turned pro and lost his first ATP match in posh Gstaad, 6–4, 6–4 on red clay in July to an Argentine player, Lucas Arnold Ker, then ranked eighty-eighth. He earned $5,250 for his efforts.

A few weeks later, he lost in the first round of a challenger event in Geneva to a Bulgarian, Orlin Stanoytchev.

In October, Roger lost to Andre Agassi, 6–3, 6–2 in the first round of the Swiss Indoors in Basel.

Weeks later, playing indoors in a satellite tournament in Küblis, Roger was fined $100 ($13 more than the $87 in prize money he earned) for lack of effort during a first-round loss to Armando Brunold.

1999	Federer notched his first Davis Cup victory (first overall and first on Swiss soil), beating Davide Sanguinetti, then ranked forty-eighth, in four sets.
	Roger earned his first ATP victories in Switzerland at the Swiss Open, beating Martin Damm and Alexander Popp, before losing to Tim Henman in the quarterfinals.
2000	Roger hooked up with Mirka at the Sydney Olympics, kissing her for the first time on the last day of the Games. They went off in separate directions as he was on the ATP tour and she the WTA tour but when they returned to Switzerland later that fall, they were a couple, though they tried to keep a low profile.
2001	After Roger's breakout win at Wimbledon over Pete Sampras, he moved into a two-room apartment near the House of Tennis in Biel with fellow Swiss tennis player Michael Lammer. According to Lammer, Mirka spent a lot of time there and made sure the place remained "reasonably clean."
2002	Roger's coach, Peter Carter, died in an auto accident in South Africa. Roger and other tennis luminaries attend his funeral at St. Leonhard's Church in Basel.

2003	Roger lost to his future coach Ivan Ljubičić in the second round of the Swiss Indoors.
	Federer won Wimbledon for the first time and honored his commitment to play at the Swiss Open in Gstaad. He was greeted at the Gstaad airport with champagne and stayed in the Suite Etoile (star suite) at the Hotel Bellevue. He lost in the final and was given Juliett, a 1,800-pound Simmental dairy cow; ten years later he was given another cow, Desiree. He played in this tournament just once more, in 2013, when he lost in the first round.
	Roger moved out of the house he shared with his parents in Bottmingen, an upscale suburb of Basel, and to an apartment he shared with Mirka in a neighboring town, Oberwil.
2004	Federer won the Swiss Open in Gstaad for the first time.
2005	A huge crowd greeted Roger in Basel's Market Square after he won Wimbledon for a third time.
2006	After not playing the event in 2004 and 2005, Federer won his first Swiss Indoors title, beating Fernando González in a third-set tiebreaker. (He also won his semifinal match that year in a third-set tiebreaker against Paradorn Srichaphan.)

2007	Roger got a stamp named after him. It was the first time the Swiss gave the honor to a living person.
2008	On April 11, Roger and Mirka married at Villa Wenkenhof, just outside Basel.
	Roger and Mirka moved from Oberwil, outside Basel, to Wollerau, a town on the west bank of Lake Zürich, just outside Zürich canton.
2009	Roger and Mirka's first set of twins, Myla and Charlene, were born at Privatklinik Bethanien hospital on July 23.
2011	In October, Federer fans launched a write-in campaign to Facebook group called "Roger Federer for Senator in the Canton of Schwyz." He received about 132 write-in votes in the first round of voting and the following month, he received about 200 more votes in the second round. (Roughly 15,000 shy of what he would have needed to win.) He made it clear that he was not interested in the office in any case.
	Swiss Federal Railways names a train after Roger. It's called The Federer Express.
2013	Roger and Mirka moved their official residence to Valbella in the Swiss Alps, where they built a magnificent home with an adjacent guest home for Roger's parents.

2014	Leo and Lenny, Roger and Mirka's second set of twins, were born on May 6.
	Roger led the Swiss Davis Cup team to its first ever championship, beating France 3–1 in the final tie.
2016	Local authorities named a street adjacent to the Swiss House of Tennis in Biel "Roger Federer Allee."
2017	Roger was awarded an honorary PhD from the Medical Faculty of the University of Basel for his lifetime contributions to the sport and to Switzerland.
2019	Roger and Mirka bought lakefront land (eighteen thousand square meters) just outside the historic village of Rapperswil, south of Zürich, with intentions to build another dream home there.
	The Swissmint introduced a twenty-franc Roger Federer coin, which shows him lining up a backhand. All thirty-three thousand sold out during the coin's "pre-sale" as some thirteen million visitors caused the website to crash at times.

Acknowledgments

Thanks to my family, Jen, Leo, and James for all the support over the years. Thanks to my mom, Joanne, and dad, Carmen, who seem to enjoy my work more than anyone else on the planet. (Or are at least great actors.) I owe all five of my big brothers—Steve, Peter, Paul, Mark, and Greg—a lot (though not any cash, at least as far as I'm aware), particularly Greg, who has purchased more copies of my books than anyone in the world.

Thanks to those who provided feedback on this manuscript, particularly Tom Swick, Megan Fernandez, Deirdre Carney, and Georgi Filipovski, who is definitely the nicest person in the Balkans, if not all of Europe or the world.

I couldn't have written this book without the help of many incredibly kind people in Switzerland. Huge thanks to Marc Dosch, Abbot Federer, Jakob and Antonia Federer, Toni Poltera, Divine Bonga, Madeleine Bärlocher, Marko Budic, Daniel Altermatt, Claudine Sommer, Anneke Geyer, Mägi Blaser, Andy Werdenberg, Rene Stauffer, Suzanne MacNeille, Amy Virshup, and Yves Allegro, among others.